THE WORDS THAT BRING US TO DANCE

THE POETRY OF HAFEZ OF SHIRAZ: THE FIRST 30 GHAZALS

ALI ARSANJANI

For my Family: B. Daftari, Eti Daftari,
Maryam Daftari, Parastoo Arsanjani, Sam Arsanjani
For the lovers of Poetry worldwide, esp. the lovers of Persian Poetry.

CONTENTS

THE WORDS THAT BRING US TO DANCE

Ali Arsanjani

Translations of the Ghazals of Hafez into English Ghazals.

ACKNOWLEDGMENTS

The author would like to especially acknowledge and express deep gratitude and indebtedness to the invaluable inspiration, masterful editing, suggestions and deep collaboration of my beloved mother , Maryam Daftari, on this and other projects, and who has been mentoring, motivating and coaching my poetry and translations for years.

Also, I would like to acknowledge the prior translators of Hafez through the long corridor of time and to the ones that will come after this one. For a list, see the references section.

PREFACE

Translating the Timeless Voice of Hafez

Translating the profound poetry of Hafez is akin to embarking on a spiritual journey. His ghazals, with their exquisite beauty and depth, resonate with readers across cultures and ages. This collection of the first thirty ghazals aims to present the essence of Hafez's work, offering both translations and detailed commentaries that unravel the layers of meaning embedded within each couplet.

Hafez, has gained the honorary title of "Lesan-al-Gheib" or "Voice of the Unmanifest" or literally, the "Tongue of the Hidden," is a poet whose work transcends the boundaries of historical epoch and culture and place. His verses are a symphony of mysticism, love, and philosophical reflection, capturing the universal quest for truth and beauty. To translate Hafez is not merely to convert words from Persian to English but to convey the spiritual and emotional resonance that his poetry invokes.

In approaching these translations, we have strived to balance between literal fidelity to the original text and the lyrical flow that would resonate with modern and English readers. Each ghazal has been translated with meticulous attention to the subtleties of the Persian language, aiming to preserve some semblance of the musicality, rhythm, and imagery that are hallmarks of Hafez's style. Our goal is to capture not only the literal meaning but also the poetic essence, the distilled meanings behind the metaphors, often alluding to Sufi or cultural innuendos; and converting some aspect of the musicality of the ghazal into English while maintaining the depth and nuance of the original.

Detailed Commentaries

Accompanying each translation is a rather detailed commentary that delves into the historical, cultural, and spiritual contexts of the poem. These commentaries are designed to illuminate the intricate tapestry of meanings woven into Hafez's verses, offering readers insights into the poet's world and the philosophical and mystical currents that influenced his work.

Sufi and Cultural Terminology

In addition to the commentary directly on the poems, the ghazals, and to enhance the reader's understanding and appreciation of Hafez's poetry, this book includes sections dedicated to explaining key Sufi and cultural terms. Sufism, with its rich tradition of metaphysical and mystical exploration, is a significant influence on Hafez's poetry. Understanding terms like "tavern," "wine," and "beloved" in their Sufi context reveals deeper layers of meaning, transforming what might seem like simple imagery into profound metaphors for spiritual truths.

Having mentioned the notion of the Sufi and related imagery and metaphors, we must remember that hafez was about 100 years after Rumi. why is this significant? because in those hundred years it can be said that the initially profound characterization of Sufism or Irfan [Erfan] as it is called in Farsi which translates directly as *knowledge* or *deep understanding*; the ability to understand or gain insights into the deeper "secrets" or "truths" of the spiritual Realm; the realm of the Unseen, the Unmanifest that underlies all of existence.

Bridging Cultures and Ages

Hafez's poetry speaks to the human condition in a language that is both specific to his time and at the same time universally relevant. By providing translations, commentaries, and cultural explanations, this book seeks to bridge the gap between Hafez's 14th-century Persian world and the modern reader. Whether you are a seasoned scholar of Persian literature or a newcomer to Hafez's work, this collection aims to offer you a meaningful encounter with one of the greatest poets of all time.

An Invitation to Reflect

As you immerse yourself in the first thirty ghazals of Hafez, we invite you to reflect not only on the surface meanings of the words but also on the deeper spiritual and philosophical questions they evoke. Let Hafez's poetry be a mirror in which you see your own soul's journey, a guide that leads you through the complexities of love, longing, and the search for divine truth.

Crafting Musicality in Translation

One of the most challenging aspects of translating Hafez's ghazals is preserving their inherent musicality. The original Persian ghazals possess a rhythm and melody that are integral to their impact. In our translations, we have endeavored to convert this musicality into English, crafting each line with attention to its sound and cadence. This effort is aimed at translating ghazals to not only convey the subtler meanings but also evoke some semblance of the emotional and aesthetic response that comes with having the refrain or radif and following a ghazal structure and assonance as much as feasible in a translation.

May these translations and commentaries bring you closer to the timeless wisdom of Hafez and enrich your understanding of his profound legacy.

With reverence and admiration for the masterful work of Hafez,

Ali Arsanjani and Maryam Daftari

CHAPTER 1
INTRODUCTION: THE LEGACY OF HAFEZ

HAFEZ, the celebrated Persian poet of the 14th century, holds a unique place in the pantheon of world literature. Known as the "Speaker of the Unmanifest," or literally, "Tongue of the Unseen", (*Lisaan-ul-ghaib*) his ghazals are revered for their profound spiritual insights, lyrical beauty, and rich symbolism. Hafez's poetry transcends the boundaries of time and place, resonating deeply with readers across diverse cultures and epochs. His verses, often infused with mysticism, love, and philosophical reflections, continue to inspire and enchant to this day.

The Structure of the Ghazal

The ghazal, a poetic form consisting of rhyming couplets and a refrain, is the medium through which Hafez meticulously has expressed his thoughts and emotions. In a mastercrafted fashion. Each couplet can stand as a self-contained unit, yet collectively, they weave a tapestry of meaning that reveals itself upon deeper layers of meaning and contemplation. We have tried to provide somewhat detailed commentary for each ghazal, as well as some explanation of terminologies that Hafez employed.The beauty of the ghazal lies in its ability to convey complex ideas through simple yet evocative language, making it a fitting vehicle for Hafez's explorations of love, spirituality, and human nature.

The Challenge of Translation

Translating Hafez's ghazals is an endeavor fraught with challenges. The Persian language, with its rich literary and cultural heritage, poses unique difficulties for translators. The nuances of Hafez's diction, the layered meanings of his words, and the musicality of his verses must all be carefully considered and hopefully, preserved to maintain the integrity of the original poems. Our approach has been to strike a delicate balance between a literal translation and one that only sounds good in English. We have aimed to capture not just the words, but the soul of Hafez's poetry.

The Difficulty in Conveying Musicality in Translation

One of the hallmarks of Hafez's ghazals is their inherent musicality. The rhythm and melody of the original Persian are integral to the emotional and aesthetic impact of his poetry. In translating these ghazals, we have endeavored to convert this musicality into English, crafting each line with careful attention to its sound and cadence. This effort ensures that the translated ghazals evoke the same emotional and aesthetic response as the originals, preserving the lyrical quality that is so central to Hafez's work.

Detailed Commentaries

To aid readers in their journey through Hafez's world, each translation is accompanied by a detailed commentary. These commentaries provide insights into the historical, cultural, and spiritual contexts of the poems, illuminating the intricate layers of meaning that Hafez weaves into his verses. In exploring the philosophical and mystical currents that most probably influenced or are related to Hafez and his worldview, readers can gain a deeper understanding of the themes and symbols in his poetry.

Sufi and Cultural Terminology

Understanding deeper layers of Hafez's poetry will be further facilitated by some familiarity with key Persian metaphors and terms; some Sufi and some cultural terms. Sufism, with its rich tradition of metaphysical and mystical exploration, is a significant influence on Hafez's work. Terms like "tavern," "wine," and "beloved" take on profound symbolic meanings in the Sufi context, transforming ordinary imagery into metaphors for spiritual truths. This book includes sections dedicated to explaining these terms, further enhancing the reader's understanding of layered meanings and paving the way for readers from all backgrounds to appreciate the layers and depth of Hafez's poetry.

Bridging Cultures and Ages

Hafez's poetry speaks to the universal human condition, addressing themes that are as relevant today as they were in the 14th century. By providing translations, commentaries, and cultural explanations, this collection aims to bridge the gap between Hafez's Persian world and the modern reader. Whether you are well-versed in Persian literature or a newcomer to Hafez's work, this book offers a meaningful encounter with one of the greatest poets of all time.

An Invitation to Reflect

As you immerse yourself in the first thirty ghazals of Hafez, I invite you to reflect not only on the surface meanings of the words but also on the deeper spiritual and philosophical questions they evoke. Let Hafez's poetry be a mirror in which you see your own soul's journey, a guide that leads you through the complexities of love, longing, and the search for divine truth as well as their interplay with the practicalities and contradictions of everyday life.

Through these translations and commentaries, may you find yourself transported into the timeless world of Hafez, discovering the profound wisdom and beauty that have captivated readers for centuries.

CHAPTER 2
THE POETIC INFLUENCE OF HAFEZ

GOETHE AND HAFEZ

JOHANN WOLFGANG VON GOETHE, the celebrated German writer, had profound admiration for the Persian poet Hafez (also spelled as Hafiz). Goethe's encounter with Hafez's poetry led him to write the "West-östlicher Divan" (West-Eastern Divan), a collection of lyrical poems that were heavily influenced by the Persian poet's works. This collection not only reflects Goethe's passion for the East and Persian poetry but also signifies a deep cultural dialogue between the East and the West.

Discovery and Influence

Goethe came across Hafez's work around 1814. The stimulus was a German translation of Hafez's ghazals. This discovery came at a time in Goethe's life when he was undergoing personal turmoil, and Hafez's poetry resonated deeply with him. This can be seen in the way the themes of love, wine, and spirituality, prevalent in Hafez's work, find their way into Goethe's "West-östlicher Divan."

The West-Eastern Divan

This collection is not just an imitation of Persian poetic forms but a true synthesis of the spirit of both Eastern and Western literary traditions. Goethe divides it into various books, with names like "The Book of the Singer," "The Book of Reflection," etc. Many of these poems engage in a direct conversation with Hafez, reflecting Goethe's attempt to internalize and continue the poetic discourse started by the Persian master.

Admiration and Kindred Spirit

Goethe saw in Hafez a kindred spirit. He famously said, "Hafez has no peer!" Through his engagement with Hafez's poetry, Goethe explored mysticism, the fleeting nature of life, and the profound depths of love, all themes that resonated with his own philosophical leanings.

Cultural Bridge

Goethe's engagement with Hafez was also significant from a cultural perspective. At a time when the East and West were often seen as dichotomous entities, Goethe's "West-östlicher Divan" served as a bridge, highlighting the universality of human experience and emotion. Goethe's work emphasized the idea that cultures could enrich one another through exchange and mutual appreciation.

Legacy

The dialogue that Goethe started with Hafez continues to this day. The "West-östlicher Divan" is seen as a seminal work that has inspired many later poets and thinkers. It has also played a role in fostering German-Persian cultural relations.

Goethe's encounter with Hafez's poetry was not a mere fleeting fascination, but a deep and transformative experience. The German poet's reverence for Hafez can be summed up in his own words: "*In his poetry, Hafez has inscribed undeniable truth, indelibly.*"Emerson and Hafez

The pathway through which Ralph Waldo Emerson discovered Hafez is noteworthy, as it underscores the interconnectedness of global literary traditions.

Goethe's "West-östlicher Divan" was a Bridge between East and West.

Emerson's introduction to Hafez was facilitated, in part, by his admiration for Johann Wolfgang von Goethe. Goethe's "West-östlicher Divan," a collection of poems heavily inspired by Hafez, served as a gateway for Emerson to delve into Persian poetry.

We can consider Goethe to be a Catalyst for Emerson. Goethe's profound respect and admiration for Hafez, evident in the "West-östlicher Divan," piqued Emerson's curiosity. Recognizing the deep philosophical resonance between Hafez's verses and Goethe's poetic interpretations, Emerson became more inclined to explore Hafez's original works.

Emerson held Goethe in high esteem, considering him one of the titans of world literature. In his essay "Goethe; or, the Writer," Emerson acknowledges Goethe's vast influence and his role in introducing Eastern thought to Western readers. This essay, while a broader exploration of Goethe's genius, also touches upon Goethe's engagement with Eastern poetry.

The bridge formed by Goethe, facilitated not just a literary appreciation, but a philosophical alignment as well. Goethe's own engagement with the themes of love, mysticism, and spirituality in the "Divan" mirrored those of Hafez. In turn, these themes resonated with Emerson's Transcendentalist beliefs. This triadic connection—Hafez, Goethe, and Emerson—created a tapestry of shared philosophies across cultures and centuries.

Goethe's "West-östlicher Divan" played a pivotal role in introducing Emerson to Hafez. While Emerson would eventually seek more direct translations and interpretations of Hafez's works, it was through Goethe's poetic lens that he first glimpsed the beauty and depth of the Persian poet's verses. This journey underscores the rich dialogues and exchanges that can occur in global literary traditions, where one great mind leads to the discovery of another across time and space.

CHAPTER 3
HAFEZ, HIS LIFE AND TIMES

HAFEZ OF SHIRAZ, or more precisely, Khwāja Shams-ud-Dīn
Muhammad Hāfez-e Shīrāzī born around 1315-1325 in Shiraz, Iran and
passed away approx 1389-1390, stands as a towering figure in Persian
literature and Sufi mysticism. Hafez, is one of the greatest poets and
ghazal writers of Iran. He spent almost his entire life in the city of his
brith, Shiraz. He was born in a neighborhood of Shiraz called "Takyeh
Mosalla" and is also buried there. His fondness for his old haunts and
unique places in the city are reflected in his poems.

His *mastery of the ghazal form, profound spiritual insights,* and *ability to
convey the complexities of love and existence* continue to captivate readers
around the world.

His legacy, rich in both cultural and literary significance, ensures
that Hafez's voice will echo through the ages, offering wisdom and
beauty to all who encounter his work.

Born in Shiraz, a city known for its vibrant cultural heritage,
Hafez's early life remains shrouded in mystery. We glean glimpses of
his formative years through his own poetry and later biographical
sources. He received a traditional Islamic education, mastering theol-
ogy, jurisprudence, and Persian literature. His designated title of
"Hafez" indicates his ability in memorizing the entire Qur'an. His

familiarity with the Qur'an shines through his work, where he weaves intricate tapestries of Qur'anic imagery and allusions.

Hafez's literary output primarily consists of ghazals, lyric poems that explore the depths of love and metaphysical longing. His *verses are characterized by their intricate wordplay, exquisite imagery, and philosophical depth*. It is known historically that he would make countless revisions until the artistry and subtlety of his poetry was to his partial satisfaction. He dances with language, creating metaphors that shimmer with multiple meanings. Take, for example, the famous line, "The tavern is a house of prayer, and the wine, a fountain of life." Here, Hafez *blurs the line between the sacred and profane*, prompting the reader to ponder the duality of existence and the potential for spiritual awakening in seemingly mundane experiences.

One of the most compelling aspects of Hafez's poetry is its amalgam of common and spiritual, scared and profane, Magi and Sufi . His ghazals frequently explore the paradoxes of spiritual and earthly love, the fleeting nature of life, and the quest for divine union. He uses wine, taverns, and beloveds as metaphors, blurring the lines between secular and sacred, sparking debates about whether his work is primarily mystical or hedonistic.

It is in the realm of love, however, that Hafez's genius truly shines. He captures the bittersweet essence of longing, the ecstasy of union, and the pain of separation. His beloved, often a symbol of the Divine, becomes a vehicle for exploring the complexities of human desire and the yearning for ultimate connection.

But Hafez's poetry is not simply a celebration of love. It delves into the darker aspects of human existence, exploring themes of loss, disappointment, and the inevitability of death. Yet, even in the face of despair, his voice remains optimistic, reminding us that within every moment lies the potential for transformation and renewal.

Themes and Style

A hallmark of Hafez's poetry is its layered complexity. His work often employs:

• **Imagery**: Rich visual and sensory details that evoke emotions and metaphysical concepts.

- **Symbolism**: Use of common objects (wine, roses, nightingales) as symbols for deeper spiritual truths.
- **Paradox and Ambiguity**: Creating multi-faceted meanings that allow for personal and mystical interpretations.
- **Metaphor**: Blending the sacred and the profane, often through the use of wine and taverns, which can symbolize divine love and spiritual intoxication.

Mysticism and Philosophy

A central aspect of Hafez's poetry is its Sufi mysticism. Sufism, the mystical branch of Islam, emphasizes the inward search for God and the renunciation of worldly desires. Hafez's ghazals frequently explore the paradoxes of spiritual and earthly love, the ephemeral nature of life, and the quest for divine union. His use of wine, taverns, and beloveds as metaphors often blurs the lines between secular and sacred, leading to debates about whether his work is primarily mystical or hedonistic.

Legacy and Influence

Hafez's influence extends far beyond the realm of Persian literature. His Divan (collected works) has been a source of inspiration for countless poets, scholars, and ordinary readers. His poetry has been translated into numerous languages, with his themes resonating universally. Goethe, the German literary giant, famously admired Hafez and was inspired by him in his own West-Eastern Divan.

In Persian culture, Hafez's poetry is deeply embedded in the fabric of daily life. His verses are often quoted in conversation, used in fortune-telling, and recited in times of celebration and sorrow. The tomb of Hafez in Shiraz, known as Hāfezieh, remains a site of pilgrimage for those who seek to honor his memory and draw inspiration from his timeless words.

Detailed Biography of Shams al-Din Mohammad, known as Hafez of Shiraz According to the Dehkhoda Dictionary & Encyclopedia

The following is a translation of the entry in the prestigious Persian encyclopedia of Dehkhoda.

According to biographers, his main title is Shams al-Din, as derived from the following couplet from a poem marking his death:

"Towards the highest paradise departed / The unique era, Shams al-Din Mohammad."

The writer of the preface to Hafez's Divan refers to him as "Shams al-Milla wa al-Din," and one of Hafez's printed Divans writes "Shams al-Din wa al-Dunya." It is evident that his title was Shams al-Din, with "Milla" and "Dunya" being additional.

After his death, admirers and mystics praised him with titles such as the Nightingale of Shiraz, Tongue of the Unseen, Master of Mysticism, Master of Shiraz, Interpreter of Truth, Revealer of Realities, Interpreter of Secrets, Enraptured Seeker, and Interpreter of Language. His name, unanimously agreed upon by biographers, is Mohammad, confirmed by the following couplet marking his death:

"The second Saadi, Mohammad Hafez / From this fleeting world went to the abode of comfort."

His pen name, Hafez, was often used in the closing verses of his ghazals and in some of his other poems. He even has a ghazal ending with the word "Hafez," starting with:

"From the evil eye, may God protect your good face / For all beauty He has placed in you, Hafez."

In the past, "Hafez" referred to those who had memorized the Quran. Hafez of Shiraz also memorized the Quran with seven narrations:

"Your love comes to the rescue if, like Hafez / You recite the Quran by heart with fourteen narrations."

Thus, he chose "Hafez" as his pen name:

"None in the world has gathered / Wisdom's subtleties and Quranic points like I have."

Family: There is no precise information about Hafez's family. His grandfather is identified as Sheikh Ghiyas al-Din, and his father as Baha al-Din, hailing from Kopay of Isfahan or Kamel al-Din from Tusirkan. There are also differing accounts regarding his father's occupation. Riaz al-Arifin claims they were scholars, while Tazkirat al-Mikhana mentions his father was a wealthy merchant.

His grandfather or father moved from their birthplace to Shiraz during the rule of the Atabaks of Fars and settled there. According to Abd al-Nabi, the author of Mikhana, his mother was from Kazeroon and lived in the Darvazeh Kazeroon neighborhood of Shiraz. After his father's death, Hafez and his two brothers lived together for a while before parting ways, with poverty befalling them. One of his brothers, whom Hafez referred to as "Khajeh Khalil Adel," likely named Khalil al-Din Adel, is remembered by Hafez in the following verses:

"His brother Khajeh Adel, may his abode be pure / After fifty-nine years of his life, He traveled to the paradise / May God be pleased with his deeds and attributes."

Given the number "Khalil Adel" in Abjad (numerical value) being 775, it marks his death year, and since his age was 59, his birth year is 716.

Hafez also composed this piece, possibly in memory of another brother who died young:

"Alas for the garment of youthful beauty / If it had the eternal embroidery, Alas, woe that from this stream / The water of life will not flow, One must cut ties / Such is the heavenly decree."

Education and Poetry: Hafez was reportedly born in Shiraz, with some writers certainly and others seemingly agreeing. Mullah Abd al-Nabi Fakhr Zamani Qazvini in Tazkirat al-Mikhana writes that his mother was from Kazeroon, living in Darvazeh Kazeroon, Shiraz. Some writers noted his residence in the Shiyadan neighborhood of Shiraz, which merged with the Mooristan neighborhood during Karim Khan Zand's era and is adjacent to Shahzadeh.

There is disagreement about Hafez's birth date. The Encyclopedia Britannica states that the exact date of his birth is unknown, but it is certainly before 700 Hijri (1320 AD). Generally, his birth is placed in the early 8th century Hijri (14th century AD). The French Encyclopedia records his birth in the first quarter of the 8th century Hijri. For example, if his death year is 791 or 792, his birth would be around 745 or 746. The author of Tazkirat al-Mikhana states his age as 65, making his birth year 726.

Hafez, according to the preface attributed to Mohammad Golandam, attended the classes of the religious leader Moulana and our master, the human teacher Qavam al-Milla wa al-Din Abdullah, and acquired knowledge from other scholars of his time. He himself said:

"The knowledge and virtue that my heart gathered in forty years / I fear that drunken narcissus will take it all at once."

He often mentioned the school and the debates:

"The arches and rooms of the school and the noise of debate / We have left behind for the wine and the fair-faced cupbearer."

He memorized the Quran:

"I did not find anything sweeter than your poetry, Hafez / By the Quran you hold within your chest."

Love for Shiraz. Hafez had a deep affection for his homeland, Shiraz, which is evident in his poetry:

"Shiraz and the water of Rukni and that pleasant breeze / Do not find fault, for it is the beauty mark of seven countries."

He also described Shiraz in his ghazals:

"Happy is Shiraz and its unmatched state / God, protect it from decline, From Ruknabad we have a hundred Allah's blessings / Which grants the life of Khidr with its clarity, Between Ja'farabad and Mosalla / The north wind comes fragranced."

Therefore, Hafez did not wish to leave Shiraz and attributed his reluctance to travel to his love for Shiraz and its scenic spots:

"They do not permit me to travel / The breeze of Mosalla and the water of Ruknabad."

However, eventually, his adversaries caused him distress, and he said:

"We have tested our luck in this city / It is time to pull our belongings out of this abyss."

He desired to travel:

"The climate of Fars strangely raises the low / Where is the companion to take the tent out of this soil?"

He eventually found an opportunity to travel to Yazd, then under the rule of Shah Yahya (nephew of Shah Shoja). Hafez expressed his affection for Yazdis in this ghazal:

"O breeze, tell the inhabitants of Yazd about us / That the ball of your mallet is your disdainful head."

After some time, Sultan Mahmud Shah Deccani invited Hafez to India. Hafez accepted and went to the island of Hormuz, boarded a ship, but adverse winds caused the sea to become turbulent. Hafez refused to proceed and disembarked, sending the following ghazal to Mirza Fazl Allah Inju, the minister of Mahmud Shah:

"Spending a moment with sorrow is worth more than the whole world / Sell my robe for wine, for nothing is better than this."

Hafez's Path. Discussions about Hafez's path are numerous. It is clear that he was long in search and wandered:

"The heart, like a compass, circled everywhere / And in that circle, it remained bewildered and steadfast."

He fell into the valley of wonder:

"Wherever I went, it added only to my confusion / Beware of this desert and this endless path."

He realized:

"This path cannot be bound by forms / For it has a hundred thousand stages at the beginning."

Hafez awaited long and said:

"I died of waiting, and there is no way in this veil / Or if there is, the keeper does not show me."

Hafez grew weary of wandering and understood that relying on oneself alone does not lead to union:

"By one's own effort, one cannot attain the gem of the goal / It is an illusion that this task can be done without divine will."

He often mentioned the need for guidance:

"Is there a person of heart to show the right way / For we did not find the path to the friend in any way."

There is a difference of opinion regarding Hafez's death. According to the most accepted view, he passed away in 792 Hijri (circa 1389 AD).

Tomb. Hafezieh is the name of Hafez's tomb in Shiraz, greatly revered by the people. Both the locals and those who come from around the world to Shiraz always consider it a place of pilgrimage. Hafez's grave is surrounded by many other graves, belonging to those who wished to be buried near the body of this spiritual man, fulfilling his verse:

"When you pass by our grave, seek a blessing / For it will be a pilgrimage site for the world's sages."

(Sourced from: Dehkhoda's Dictionary)

CHAPTER 4
CONTRASTS AND SIMILARITIES BETWEEN RUMI AND HAFEZ

MOLANA **Rumi**

Jalāl ad-Dīn Muhammad Mowlavi Balkhi Rūmī, commonly known as Rumi, was another towering figure in Persian poetry and Sufism, born a century earlier in 1207. While both Hafez and Rumi are celebrated for their contributions to Persian literature and mysticism, their styles, themes, and approaches offer fascinating contrasts. Let's explore some of them (see digital resources , [3])

Themes and Philosophy

Rumi: His poetry is profoundly spiritual, focusing on the soul's relationship with the divine. Rumi's works often center on themes of divine love, the soul's journey towards God, and the transcendent nature of the spiritual path.

Hafez: While also deeply spiritual, Hafez's poetry often explores the tension between the sacred and the profane. His ghazals can be read on multiple levels—romantic, philosophical, and mystical—highlighting the duality of human experience.

Style and Expression

Rumi: Known for his Masnavi, a six-book spiritual epic, Rumi's style is direct and didactic, aimed at guiding the reader towards spiritual enlightenment. His use of storytelling and allegory is prominent.

Hafez: Hafez's style is more lyrical and enigmatic. His ghazals are shorter, densely packed with symbolism and layered meanings. The ambiguity in his poetry invites multiple interpretations, making it both a literary and mystical puzzle.

Literary Approach

Rumi: His works often read as instructional and expository, with a clear emphasis on conveying spiritual lessons. Rumi's poetry tends to be more expansive and narrative-driven.

Hafez: Hafez's ghazals are more condensed and poetic, focusing on the beauty of language and the evocation of complex emotions. His approach is less didactic and more contemplative, allowing the reader to derive personal insights.

Rumi's poetry often reflects a more directly spiritual, direct communion, ecstatic and devotional approach, characterized by its direct and passionate expression of divine love. His imagery is vivid and evocative, often focusing on the mystic's journey towards union with the Beloved.

Hafez, on the other hand, is known for his being a *Rend*, and an accomplished Ghazalian Poet; with intricate wordplay, complex metaphors, and the exploration of the ambiguities of mostly earthly love. *His ghazals often delve into the paradoxes of human desire, the struggles of the soul, and the search for meaning within the complexities of everyday life.*

While both poets offer profound insights into the human condition and the nature of the Divine, their unique styles and approaches to Sufism provide distinct perspectives on the mystic's journey. *Hafez, with his intricate wordplay and focus on the complexities of love, reminds us of the beauty and ambiguity inherent in human experience, while Rumi's passionate and direct voice calls us towards a more experiential and deeper connection with the Beloved.*

Hafez's poetry, like the wine he so often uses as a metaphor, is both intoxicating and thought-provoking. It invites us to savor each moment, to embrace the paradoxes of life, and to search for meaning in the beauty and ambiguity that surrounds us.

Hafez of Shiraz and Rumi both made indelible marks on Persian literature and Sufi mysticism, yet their distinct approaches offer unique windows into the spiritual and poetic traditions of their time. Hafez's lyrical ambiguity and Rumi's direct spiritual guidance together enrich the tapestry of Persian poetic heritage, each providing profound insights into the human quest for meaning and divine connection.

The God of Rumi vs. The God of Hafez [See Soroush, Digital Resources, 3]: Contrasting Perspectives

Both Rumi and Hafez are giants in Persian literature and Sufi mysticism, yet their conceptions of God and the divine relationship exhibit significant differences that reflect their unique worldviews.

Rumi's Conception of God

Intimate and Personal: Rumi's God is deeply personal and accessible, fostering a direct and intimate relationship with the believer. This is evident in Rumi's poetry, where God is often depicted as the Beloved, a constant companion in the soul's journey.

Unity and Love: Central to Rumi's thought is the idea of Tawhid (oneness of God). He emphasizes the unity of all existence and the importance of divine love as the driving force of the universe. This love transcends the physical world and draws the believer closer to the divine.

Guidance and Instruction: Rumi's poetry often serves as a guide for spiritual seekers, offering wisdom and insights on how to attain closeness to God. His Masnavi is a prime example, filled with parables and stories that illustrate the path to spiritual enlightenment.

Hafez's Conception of God

Ambiguous and Elusive: Hafez's depiction of God is more ambiguous and often shrouded in mystery. His poetry reflects a God that is both near and far, accessible yet hidden. This ambiguity allows for a wide range of interpretations, from orthodox to heretical.

Divine Love and Worldly Beauty: While Hafez also speaks of divine love, his work frequently blurs the line between the sacred and the profane. The beloved in Hafez's poetry can represent both a divine figure and a worldly lover, reflecting the complexity of human and divine relationships.

Skeptical and Critical: Hafez's poetry often carries a tone of skepticism towards religious formalism and hypocrisy. He critiques the self-righteousness of clerics and the superficial piety of society, advocating for a more sincere and personal spiritual experience.

Difference in Worldviews

Rumi's Worldview

Optimistic and Affirmative: Rumi's worldview is inherently optimistic. He sees the world as a manifestation of divine love, where every experience, joyful or painful, is a step towards spiritual growth and unity with God.

Transcendental and Mystical: Rumi focuses on transcending the material world to achieve a higher state of spiritual awareness. His poetry encourages detachment from worldly concerns and a focus on the eternal.

Hafez's Worldview

Realistic and Critical: Hafez presents a more realistic and sometimes critical view of the world. He acknowledges the imperfections and contradictions of life and spirituality, often highlighting the flaws and hypocrisy within religious institutions.

Interplay of Sacred and Profane: Hafez's poetry reflects a deep engagement with the material world, seeing it as a mirror for the divine. He celebrates beauty, love, and wine, suggesting that these worldly experiences can also lead to spiritual insights.

The contrasting views of Rumi and Hafez on God and the divine relationship highlight the rich diversity within Persian Sufi poetry. Rumi's intimate, loving, and transcendental approach offers a path of spiritual optimism and unity, while Hafez's ambiguous, critical, and worldly engagement provides a more nuanced and realistic exploration of the divine.

CHAPTER 5
HAFEZ AND OTHER MAJOR POETS AND WRITERS

HAFEZ'S *poetic influence has traversed centuries and borders*, touching the hearts and minds of numerous poets around the world. While Goethe and Emerson are among the most prominent figures to acknowledge this influence, several other poets have also expressed their admiration for Hafez or shown traces of his influence in their work.

Friedrich Schiller, a German poet, philosopher, and playwright, was contemporaneous with Goethe. The deep interest in Oriental poetry that spread in Germany during their time led to an appreciation of Hafez's work. Schiller's fascination with themes of freedom and love tend to align with Hafezian motifs.

August von Platen, a German poet, openly expressed his admiration for Hafez. His style and themes, especially in his ghazals, reveal a Hafezian influence.

Gertrude Bell the famous English writer, traveler, and archaeologist, translated some of Hafez's works into English. Her engagement with his poetry goes beyond mere translation, with traces of Hafez's ethos appearing in her own writings.

Pablo Neruda's work was influenced by a range of experiences and readings, but he expressed special admiration for Persian poetry, including the work of Hafez. Neruda's poetry, which often blends sensual and mystical elements, has thematic parallels with Hafez's verses.

It's worth noting that while many poets have been directly influenced by Hafez, *countless others have been touched indirectly through the broader currents* of Sufi thought, Persian poetic traditions, and the universal themes that Hafez so eloquently expressed. **Ezra Pound and T.S. Eliot** had an interest in Eastern philosophy and literature, and while direct links to Hafez might be subtler than with poets like Emerson, their openness to global poetic traditions means that they were *likely aware* of and influenced by Hafez's universal themes.

Mohammad Iqbal was a philosopher, poet, and politician in British colonial India, had a profound respect for Hafez. Iqbal's poetry, which delves into themes of self-realization, freedom, and connection with the divine, resonates with Hafezian motifs.

Allameh Tabatabai was an influential Persian religious scholar and philosopher. Tabatabai wrote a commentary on Hafez's poetry, reflecting deep engagement and resonance with the Persian master's verses.

CHAPTER 6
PERSIAN MASTERS OF THE GHAZAL

NUMEROUS POETS HAVE ENRICHED the Persian ghazal tradition, but Rumi and Hafez hold a special place as two of its most celebrated and influential figures.

Rumi (13th century) **or Molana Jalal-e-din Mohammad Balkhi Rumi** was an erudite scholar who was a dean of a very major university in his time, turned Sufi mystic and spiritual teacher. Rumi's ghazals in his *Divan e Shams-e-Tabrizi,* (literally, the Divan or compilation of the poems of Shams of Tabriz) ghazals written in honor of his master, Shams of Tabriz – are renowned for their passionate expression of divine love, ecstatic longing for union with the Beloved, and profound insights into the nature of the soul. His verses employ vivid metaphors and to the uninitiated, often appearing as paradoxical language, that invites the reader – or listener as is many the case for the oral reading tradition where poems were read out loud, not just read silently – on a transformative journey of self-discovery and spiritual awakening.

Saadi Shirazi (13th century): Renowned for his wisdom and philosophical insights, Saadi's ghazals often delve into the themes of love, morality, and social justice. His verses are characterized by their clarity, eloquence, and profound understanding of human nature.

Amir Khusrau (13th-14th centuries): A pioneer in blending Persian and Indian cultural elements, Amir Khusrau's ghazals are known for their musicality, playful language, and innovative use of imagery.

Hafez (14th century) **of Shiraz or Khajeh Hafez Shirazi,** is well known for his supreme lyrical mastery of the ghazal with multiple levels of meaning and enigmatic verses. Hafez's ghazals explore the complexities of human love, the fleeting nature of earthly pleasures, and the enduring quest for meaning in life. His poetry is rich in symbolism, drawing upon imagery of wine, the tavern, and the beloved to evoke themes of spiritual intoxication and the union of the human and divine.

Beyond these luminaries, other very notable poets have also made significant contributions to the Persian ghazal tradition. Some of these luminaries include:

Jami (15th century): A Sufi mystic and scholar, Jami's ghazals are imbued with spiritual depth and philosophical contemplation, exploring the mysteries of divine love and the complexities of the human soul.

Mirza Ghalib (19th century): A master of both Urdu and Persian poetry, Ghalib's ghazals are renowned for their wit, irony, and philosophical musings, often expressing a sense of existential angst and the bittersweet nature of life.

Muhammad Iqbal (20th century): A philosopher and poet, Iqbal's ghazals are imbued with a sense of national identity and spiritual awakening, calling for social reform and the revitalization of Islamic thought.

The works of these master poets, along with countless others, have woven a rich tapestry of human experience, spiritual longing, and philosophical contemplation, making the Persian ghazal a timeless and enduring form of artistic expression.

CHAPTER 7
THE GHAZAL FORM

HISTORICAL PERSPECTIVE

THE GHAZAL IS a poetic form with deep roots in Arabic, Persian, Urdu, and Hindi literature. Its origins trace back to 7th-century Arabic poetry, but evolving and flourishing in Persian literature in the 10th century and later becoming a significant form in Urdu and other South Asian languages. This form is characterized by its unique structure, thematic depth, and stylistic elements, making it a captivating and challenging genre for poets even today. Let's delve into the principles of writing a ghazal below.

PRINCIPLES OF WRITING A GHAZAL: A DETAILED EXPLORATION

Six Structures of the Ghazal

1. Matla (Opening Couplet): The ghazal begins with a *matla*, the opening couplet where both lines rhyme and share the same meter. This sets the tone and structure for the entire poem. The *matla* is crucial because it introduces the rhyme scheme and refrain that will follow throughout the ghazal.

Example: "In the garden of my heart, a rose blooms bright,
In each petal's fold, a hidden delight."

In this example, "bright" and "delight" create the rhyme, and the meter remains consistent across both lines.

2. Radif (Refrain): The radif is a repeated word or phrase at the end of the second line of every couplet. This refrain creates a sense of continuity and musicality. The consistency of the radif provides a rhythmic anchor for the ghazal.

Example: "The moon whispers secrets to **the night,**

Stars listen quietly, in **the night.**"

Here, "[in] the night" is the radif, creating a soothing repetition and emphasizing the theme.

Note, this can be just a rhyme at the end of a word or a phrase.

3. Qafia (Rhyme): The qafia is the rhyming pattern that appears *before* the radif in each couplet. The rhyme scheme, combined with the radif, creates a melodic quality that is essential to the ghazal.

Example: "In dreams, I wander lost, **searching** in the night,

For shadows of your love, **yearning** in the night."

The words "searching" and "yearning" serve as the qafia, enhancing the lyrical flow.

4. Maqta (Final Couplet): The maqta is the final couplet of the ghazal, often containing the poet's pen name (takhallos). This personal touch allows the poet to reflect on their identity or the overarching themes of the ghazal.

Example: "Ali's heart remains a garden, blooming in the night,

With each passing dream, flowers consume the night."

Here, the poet "Ali" integrates his name into the closing lines, adding a signature flourish.

5. Bahr (Meter): Each line of the ghazal must follow the same metrical pattern or *bahr*. This uniformity in rhythm is crucial for maintaining the poem's musicality and cohesiveness.

Example: "Silent whispers in the breeze, carry tales untold,

Through the valleys and the hills, mysteries unfold."

The consistent meter across these lines ensures a harmonious flow.

6. Takhallos (Alluding to the poet; pen name or name): The poet's pen name (*takhallos*) is found in the *maqta* – the final couplet of the ghazal. This personal touch allows the poet to reflect on their identity or on their behalf on the overarching theme(s) of the ghazal.

Example: "Ali's heart remains a garden, blooming in the night,
With each passing dream, flowers consume the night."

7. **Unfolding Layers of Meaning in Successive Couplets**: In the Ghazal structure, each couplet tends to add a layer of meaning, starting from a simple instance emphasizing the transformative power of spiritual practices, the importance of kindness and patience, and the ultimate quest for divine union amidst overwhelming feelings.

CHAPTER 8
HOW TO WRITE A GHAZAL

HERE IS *an original ghazal by the author on how to write a ghazal.*

HOW TO WRITE A GHAZAL

Rumi, Hafez, Saadi, and others have already contained what I write
    I pay respect to these masters, so they may ordain what I write

I choose an opening, a theme of love and I use a *radif*, a refrain that I write
    For every second couplet line, to a pre-*radif* rhyme I train what I write

In five to seventeen stanzas I try to weave the story, gently tight
    To lend a shape to formless love, so *it* can explain what I write

I dip into our cherished memories caught in the rainbow web of time
    And paint deep colors, that dispel doubt, of why I can claim what I write

. . .

Longing of love, mystic union, desire and doubt, all run out of words
  As the Inexpressible whispers to me, I can barely contain what I write

With that, I explore dark corners of love powered by the longing of the reed
  Don't ask! I am burdened with secrets to keep; so I have to constrain what I write

This love is a promise that was made under the moonlight, in another millenium
  Its freshness lasts-- I am eager to explain, if only you would retain what I write

Mystic Lover, my hope is lavender dew that will soon be lost to the sun
  Recount the lovestory of the rose and nightingale, so it ascertains what I write

Lastly, I refer to myself -- a *takhalos*, at the last couplet of the *ghazal*
  I package the moral in a drop of dew, then pray that I can attain what I write

CHAPTER 9
COMMON THEMES AND STYLES OF THE GHAZAL

HERE ARE some common themes that ghazals have been written to represent, over time.

1. Love and Longing: Ghazals often explore themes of love, both earthly and divine. The intense emotions of longing and unfulfilled desire are central, reflecting the poet's inner world.

Example: "In your absence, my heart yearns, an endless night,

In the shadow of your memory, I find light."

The poet expresses profound longing and the paradox of finding light in the darkness of memory.

2. Mysticism and Spirituality: Many ghazals delve into mystical themes, portraying the poet's quest for spiritual enlightenment and connection with the divine.

Example: "With each breath, I seek your presence, a sacred rite,

In the silence of my soul, you ignite light."

The poet's spiritual journey is depicted as a sacred, ongoing quest.

3. Beauty and Nature: Descriptions of beauty, whether of a beloved or the natural world, are common. These images often serve as metaphors for deeper emotional states.

Example: "In the garden's bloom, your beauty finds its sight,

Each flower whispers secrets of your light."

The natural imagery reflects the beloved's beauty and the emotional resonance it carries.

4. Loss and Sorrow: Themes of loss and melancholy are prevalent, underscoring the transient nature of life and relationships.

Example: "In the echo of your laughter, silence claims its right,

Memories linger, shadows in the light."

The juxtaposition of laughter and silence captures the poignancy of loss.

SOME STYLES OF THE GHAZAL

1. Imagery and Symbolism: Ghazals rely heavily on vivid imagery and symbolic language to evoke emotions and convey deeper meanings often in a series of layered symbols that culminate in the divine connection.

"A single tear, a pearl in the ocean's might,

Reflecting worlds within, a universe of light."

The imagery of a tear as a pearl symbolizes profound emotions and the vastness of the inner world.

2. Ambiguity and Complexity: The language of a ghazal is often layered with multiple meanings, allowing for varied interpretations.

"In the mirror of your eyes, I see my plight,

A dance of shadows and dreams, veiled in light."

The ambiguity in the imagery encourages multiple interpretations of the poet's plight.

3. Couplet Independence: Each couplet (sher) in a ghazal is an independent unit, capable of standing alone while still contributing to the overall theme and mood of the poem.

"Under the moon's gaze, hearts entwine tight,

In the stillness of the night, whispers take flight."

Each couplet tells its own story yet fits into the broader tapestry of the ghazal.

4. Repetition and Variation: The use of repetition, particularly through the radif and qafia, creates a rhythmic and musical quality, while variations in imagery and themes add richness and depth.

"Through the corridors of time, memories take flight,

In the echoes of your name, I find my light."

The repetition of "flight" and "light" creates a rhythmic pattern, while the imagery continues to evolve.

The above principles allow us to, and provide guidelines for us to, craft ghazals that resonate with emotional intensity, lyrical beauty, and increasingly profound depth. The ghazal's rich history and intricate form continue — to inspire poets and readers like you — until today, a form and depth that transcends cultural and linguistic boundaries as we resonate with its rhythmic and thematic flow.

CHAPTER 10
THE LATENT MEANINGS OF PERSIAN POETRY

IN PERSIAN POETRY, especially in the works of poets like Hafez and Rumi, phrases are laden with symbolism and can be interpreted in various ways depending on the context and the reader's perspective and ultimately, their level of consciousness. For example love can be interpreted to pertain to child's love of his toys or pet, a child's love for her parents, a teenager's infatuation of another, a young person in a relationship, love of family, love of friends, love of fame, love of country, and ultimately love of God, the Divine love. These levels of interpretation often encourage contemplation and reflection on both material and spiritual matters, inviting readers to explore the deeper dimensions of existence and the path to spiritual enlightenment.

In each section, the Persian ghazal has been presented, then the English translation (in English ghazal form), then a commentary on the English translation. Note that the selection of the radif is extremely personal and you may have selected a different radif for that particular poem. What has been done was to select a radif that was thought to reflect more of the essence of what the poet is trying to communicate, based on the emphasis he has placed within the poem.

CHAPTER 11
REND: UNDERSTANDING KEY TERMS IN PERSIAN MYSTICAL POETRY

THE WORLD of Persian mystical poetry is rich with nuanced terms that carry deep spiritual and cultural significance. To appreciate the full depth of this poetry, it's essential to understand these key terms and their connotations. Let's explore terms like "رندی" (rendi), "دیر مُغان" (dair-e mughān), "شرابِ ناب" (sharāb-e nāb), "صومعه" (ṣauwme'e), and "خرقۀ سالوس" (khirqa-ye ṣāluṣ), along with their historical context and symbolic meanings.

THE REND : "رندی" (RENDI) AND "رند" (REND)

The Meaning & Connotations of a Rend: The terms "رندی" (rendi) and "رند" (rend) are crucial in Persian mystical poetry, especially in the works of poets like Hafez. These words are multifaceted and challenging to translate directly into English due to their rich cultural and literary context.

Historical Context of the Rend: Originating from Persian Sufi traditions, these terms challenge both societal and religious norms, urging readers to seek spiritual truths beyond superficial practices. Hafez, among others, used these terms to critique societal hypocrisy and emphasize genuine spiritual experiences over mere ritualistic observance.

At the Basic Level - the Rend was an Outward Nonconformist: At the most basic level, "رند" refers to someone who defies societal norms, often engaging in behavior considered immoral by orthodox standards, such as drinking wine or frequenting taverns.

In a literal sense, a rend might be seen as a libertine, someone who rejects conventional morality.

At the Deeper Level - the Rend was deeply Spiritual but a Nonconformist: On a mystical level, a "رند" is someone who, while appearing irreligious or nonconformist outwardly, understands the essence of spirituality deeply. This person often acts against societal norms to expose the hypocrisy or superficiality of mainstream religious practices.

A rend might frequent taverns not for the love of wine but to symbolize their disdain for hollow religious formalism.

The Mystical Context - the Rend as a Spiritual Insider: In Sufi poetry, a "رند" is often depicted as possessing secret knowledge and insights into divine mysteries. They comprehend the impermanence of worldly life and live by a different set of spiritual priorities.

It is unclear whether Hafez's rend might actually drink wine, unthought of in earlier times, in order to, for example, symbolize their spiritual intoxication or communion with the Divine. Living in a different time, almost 100 years after Rumi, the notion of Divinity, Piety and Abstinence began to carry different connotations; and were somewhat diluted by the passage of time and the possible gradual facetiousness that tends to set in, in most if not all religious systems over time.

Symbolic Figure: In Hafez's poetry, the Rend "رند" symbolizes authentic spiritual experience in contrast to hollow religious formalism. Their actions, like drinking wine, are metaphors for spiritual ecstasy and intimate connection with the Divine.

In many of Hafez's ghazals, the rend represents the true seeker of spiritual truths, often juxtaposed against the hypocritical orthodox.

Pious Hedonists (Rendan-e Parsa): The term "رندان پارسا" combines two seemingly contradictory qualities—piety and hedonism. In Sufi poetry, this oxymoron is often used to describe individuals who outwardly appear worldly or irreverent but are inwardly devout and spiritually advanced. This reflects a fundamental Sufi belief that external appearances can be deceiving, and true spirituality is hidden in the heart. For example, see ghazal 5.

THE TAVERN AND WINE: "دیرِ مُغان" (DAIR-E MUGHĀN) AND "شرابِ ناب" (SHARĀB-E NĀB)

دیرِ مُغان (Dair-e Mughān): This term combines "دیر" (dair), meaning "monastery," and "مُغان" (mughān), refers to Zoroastrian priests or the Magi. Together, "دیرِ مُغان" refers to a Zoroastrian temple or monastery. In Sufi poetry, it can also symbolize a tavern or winehouse, equating the act of consuming wine with seeking spiritual ecstasy and divine love.

Visiting "دیرِ مُغان" is akin to seeking spiritual enlightenment in a place of divine communion.

شرابِ ناب (Sharāb-e Nāb): This term combines "شراب" (sharab), meaning "wine," and "ناب" (nāb), meaning "pure" or "exquisite." "شرابِ ناب" thus refers to "exquisite wine" or "pure wine." In Sufi poetry, wine symbolizes divine love or spiritual ecstasy.

The intoxication from "شرابِ ناب" represents the overwhelming passion and spiritual intoxication one feels from divine love.

Combined Symbolism: When combined, "دیرِ مُغان و شرابِ ناب" conjures the image of a sacred place where one finds the intoxicating drink of divine love, symbolizing the passionate and overwhelming nature of spiritual pursuit.

Poets like Hafez use these terms to convey the idea that the spiritual quest can be as consuming as a fervent romantic endeavor.

THE MONASTERY AND THE CLOAK: "صومعه" (ṢAWMA'A) AND "خِرقۀ سالوس" (KHIRQA-YE ṢĀLUṢ)

صومعه (Ṣawma'a): This term refers to a "hermitage" or "monastery," a secluded place where ascetics and monks dedicate themselves to worship, prayer, and meditation, retreating from worldly distractions to engage in deep spiritual practices.

A ṣawma'a in Persian mystical poetry symbolizes a place of spiritual seclusion and intense devotion.

خِرقهٔ سالوس (Khirqe-ye Ṣāluṣ): This term combines "خِرقه" (kherqe), meaning a "patched cloak" worn by Sufi mystics, symbolizing renunciation of worldly possessions and humility, with "سالوس" (ṣāluṣ), meaning "piety" or "devotion." Together, it signifies the "robe of piety."

The khirqa-ye ṣāluṣ represents the spiritual garb of a devout ascetic, emphasizing a life of simplicity and spiritual dedication.

Combined Imagery: The terms "صومعه و خِرقهٔ سالوس" paint a picture of an ascetic life dedicated to spiritual practices and inner reflection, often used in Persian mystical poetry to describe an earnest spiritual seeker.

This imagery evokes a person who has renounced worldly distractions to fully commit to a spiritual path.

CHAPTER 12
GHAZAL 1: LOVE SEEMED SO EASY

اَلا یا اَیُّهَا السّاقی اَدِرْ کَأْساً و ناوِلْها
که عشق آسان نمود اوّل ولی افتاد مشکلها

به بویِ نافه‌ای کآخر صبا زان طُرّه بگشاید
ز تابِ جَعدِ مشکینش چه خون افتاد در دلها

مرا در منزلِ جانان چه امنِ عیش چون هر دَم
جَرَس فریاد می‌دارد که بَربندید مَحمِلها

به مِی سجّاده رنگین کن گرت پیر مُغان گوید

که سالِک بی‌خبر نَبوَد ز راه و رسمِ منزل‌ها

شبِ تاریک و بیمِ موج و گردابی چنین هایل
کجا دانند حالِ ما سبکبارانِ ساحل‌ها

همه کارم ز خودکامی به بدنامی کشید آخر
نهان کِی مانَد آن رازی کزو سازند محفل‌ها

GHAZAL 1: LOVE SEEMED SO EASY

My dear *Saghi*! Pour the wine and bring it around, for, at first, love seemed so easy,
  Now difficulties abound, though in the beginning, love seemed so easy

The morning breeze has unlocked the fragrance of those tresses at last.
  How much blood has been spilled by the musk of those curls, when love seemed so easy?

In the house of the Beloved, how can I ever find peace,
  for at every moment bells might toll, to pack belongings, and yet love seemed so easy.

Paint your prayer rug red with wine, if the *Magian* elder directs you to,
  For the true seeker is not unaware, of the ways of the quest, even when love seemed so easy

A dark night – the fear of waves – and such an ominous vortex,
  How can the unburdened on shore, fathom the love that seemed so easy?

All my self-centered deeds, have led in the end, to my infamy.

Is the secret hidden, when it's the gossip of assemblies? Love seemed so easy.

CHAPTER 13
SAGHI: COMMENTARY ON TERMINOLOGY

HAFEZ IS RENOWNED for his verses that effortlessly intertwine the secular with the mystical, the worldly with the divine. To appreciate Hafez's poetry and the notion of "*saghi*" within it, it's essential to have a basic grasp of Sufism and its symbolism.

The notion of "*saghi*" in Hafez's poetry and Sufism more broadly is rich with symbolic meanings, serving as a bridge between the earthly and the divine. Through this metaphor, Hafez and other Sufi poets invite readers to delve deeper into their own spiritual journeys, to question, to seek, and to experience the intoxication of divine love.

Sufism, often described as Islamic mysticism, delves deep into the esoteric, spiritual aspects of Islam, emphasizing personal experiences with the divine, self-purification, and the perfectibility of the human soul. Sufi poets, including *Rumi, Saadi, and Hafez*, often employed symbols, metaphors, and allegories to convey profound spiritual truths.

Saghi, In its literal sense, refers to a wine pourer or cupbearer or as we might refer to the role today, a kind of a bartender. In traditional Persian settings, this was often a young, beautiful person who served wine to guests. But in Sufi poetry, especially that of Hafez, "saghi" has layered symbolic meanings. Saghi in the context of the *Hafezry* of Hafez, Rumi and other Persian mystical poets signifies a range of meanings, layers of semantics, ranging from the Divine Beloved, a Spiritual Guide like a Tavern Sage, an intermediary that looks of this world but may not be, and lastly a reference to the transience of the world and its pleasures.

The Divine Beloved. In many poems, the *saghi* symbolizes God or the Divine, offering the wine of knowledge, love, and spiritual ecstasy. The wine here isn't the material drink but the intoxication of divine love and awareness.

Spiritual Guide. The *saghi* can also represent a spiritual master or guide who provides seekers with wisdom and guidance, leading them on the path toward union with the divine.

Transient Nature of Worldly Pleasures. While the beauty and allure of the *saghi* are undeniable, this figure may also serve as a reminder of the fleeting nature of worldly attractions. Such pleasures, while intoxicating, are temporary, and the true seeker should aim for the eternal love of the Divine.

Intermediary. Just as the saghi serves wine to the drinker, he can be seen as an intermediary between the human soul and God, providing sustenance and ecstasy.

Hafez and Saghi. Hafez's ghazals refer frequently to the saghi, the tavern, the tavern sage, wine, and the beloved. For Hafez, the tavern is often a place where social hierarchies dissolve, where the pious and the sinner come together, all in search of spirituality, and ultimately of a different kind of intoxication: divine intoxication. The saghi, in this setting, becomes an emblematic figure, embodying both the entice-ments of the world and the profound spiritual truths that lie beyond it.

Hafez's use of wine, tavern, and saghi imagery was unorthodox, and highly provocative in his day and age; even today might still be so in many traditional Islamic settings. By employing such symbols, he challenged conventional notions of piety, morality, and the pursuit of the divine and like Rumi before him sought to cast the spiritual experi-ence in light of analogies that transcend common terminology and even experiences; thus reaching into another domain explain spiritual experience with the aim of "showing and not telling" because it is an experience that is not conveyable within words . For Hafez, true spiri-tual seeking went beyond ritualistic practices and societal norms.

In a mystical or Sufi context, "secret" often refers to the hidden truths or mysteries of existence, and "gatherings" can allude to spiritual assemblies where seekers come together in remembrance of the Divine or in pursuit of spiritual knowledge. The last couplet in the ghazal suggests a powerful secret or truth that becomes the focal point or reason for gatherings that could be either such spiritual gatherings or ones of public gossip and leaves the reader to decide.

CHAPTER 14
GHAZAL 2: VAST DISTANCES I FIND

صلاحِ کار کجا و منِ خراب کجا
ببین تفاوتِ رہ کز کجاست تا به کجا

دلم ز صومعه بگرفت و خرقهٔ سالوس
کجاست دیرِ مُغان و شرابِ ناب کجا

چه نسبت است بهرندی صَلاح و تقوا را
سماعِ وعظ کجا نغمهٔ رباب کجا

ز رویِ دوست، دلِ دشمنان چه دریابد

چراغِ مرده کجا شمعِ آفتاب کجا

چو کُحلِ بینشِ ما خاکِ آستانِ شماست
کجا رویم بفرما ازین جناب کجا

مبین به سیبِ زَنَخدان که چاه در راه است
کجا همی رَوی ای دل بدین شتاب کجا

بشد که یاد خوشش باد روزگارِ وصال
خود آن کرشمه کجا رفت و آن عِتاب کجا

قرار و خواب ز حافظ طمع مدار ای دوست
قرار چیست صبوری کدام و خواب کجا

GHAZAL 2: VAST DISTANCES I FIND

Here, the path of wisdom; there, wretched me, in this gap, vast distances I find
  Within the tortuous paths from here to there, vast distances I find

My heart is weary of the temple and the clergy's pious robe,
  Where is the mystics' Haven, and the pure wine? To them, vast distances I find

How is conformance and piety related to the wisdom of the *Rend*
  Between a sermon's chant and the lute's melody, vast differences I find

What can the heart of an enemy feel when it sees the Face of the Beloved's grace?
  Between the eyes of the dead and bright sun's rays, vast differences I find

When the eye shade of our insight is the dust of Your threshold,
  From this esteemed place, where should we go? Tell us, for vast distances I find

Beware the allure of the rosy round cheeks; where pitfalls reside,

O heart, with such haste to which realm are you heading, for vast distances I find

Those blessed moments of closeness feel like a distant memory I miss.

Where are those flirtatious glances and reproaches now? vast distances I find

Dear friend, don't begrudge peace and sleep from Hafez!

Between peace, patience and sleep's embrace, vast distances I find

CHAPTER 15
COMMENTARY

THIS GHAZAL BY Hafez is a profound reflection on the vast distances—both literal and metaphorical—that separate different states of being, paths of life, and levels of spiritual understanding. Each couplet (*sher*) delves into contrasts between external piety and internal truth, worldly distractions and spiritual enlightenment, and past moments of joy versus present longing. Let's explore each couplet in detail.

1. The Path of Wisdom

"The path of wisdom here, and there the wretched me, in this gap, vast distances I find.

The difference in paths is from here to there, vast distances I find."

Hafez begins by highlighting the vast chasm between his current state and the path of wisdom. The "path of wisdom" signifies spiritual enlightenment and truth, while the "wretched me" represents his own perceived shortcomings or worldly entanglements. The repeated phrase "vast distances I find" emphasizes the immense struggle and distance between his current state and the ideal of wisdom. This sets the tone for the rest of the ghazal, which explores various forms of separation and contrast.

2. Weary Heart

"My heart is weary of the temple and the monk's pious robe,

Where is the mystics' Haven, and the pure wine? Vast distances I find."

In this couplet, Hafez expresses disillusionment with outward displays of piety and religious formalism, symbolized by the temple and the monk's robe. He yearns for the "mystics' Haven" and "pure wine," which represent genuine spiritual experiences and divine love. The "vast distances" here signify the gap between superficial religious practice and true mystical experience. The imagery of the temple and the robe contrasts sharply with the haven and the wine, underscoring the poet's preference for heartfelt spirituality over empty rituals.

3. Wisdom and Piety

"How is conformance and piety related to the wisdom of the Sage (Rend)?

Between sermon's chant and the lute's melody, vast distances I find."

Hafez questions the relationship between outward piety and the wisdom of the rend, a figure representing true spiritual insight. The "sermon's chant" symbolizes conventional religious teachings, while the "lute's melody" represents the soulful and direct experience of the divine. The "vast distances" here highlight the profound difference between formal religious observance and the deeper, more joyful wisdom of the mystic.

4. Enemy's Heart

"What can the heart of an enemy benefit (feel) from the Face of the Beloved's grace?

Between the eyes of the dead and bright sun's ray, vast distances I find."

Hafez contrasts the "heart of an enemy" with the "Face of the Beloved's grace." He suggests that an enemy's heart, filled with malice and blindness, cannot perceive or benefit from the divine grace. This is akin to the difference between the lifeless eyes of the dead and the vibrant rays of the sun. The "vast distances" again emphasize the insurmountable gap between spiritual blindness and enlightenment.

5. The Esteemed Place

"When the eye shade of our insight is the dust of Your threshold,

From this esteemed place, where should we go? Tell us, for vast distances I find."

Here, Hafez metaphorically describes his spiritual insight as "the dust of Your threshold," indicating utmost humility and reverence at the feet of the divine. He questions where else he could go from this esteemed place of spiritual surrender. The "vast distances" underscore the futility of seeking spiritual fulfillment elsewhere, highlighting the singular importance of divine connection.

6. The Apple of the Cheek

"Do not look at the apple of the cheek, for there's a pitfall in the way,

Where are you heading so hastily, O heart? To where?"

Hafez warns against being enticed by superficial beauty ("the apple of the cheek"), which can lead to pitfalls and distractions on the spiritual path. He questions his heart's haste, asking where it is heading. This reflects the internal struggle to stay focused on true spiritual goals amidst worldly temptations. The repeated question emphasizes the confusion and urgency in seeking the right path.

7. Rosy Cheeks

"Beware the allure of the rosy round cheeks; where pitfalls reside,

O heart, with such haste to which realm are you heading, vast distances I find."

This couplet mirrors the previous one, reinforcing the warning against being seduced by physical beauty, which symbolizes earthly desires. Hafez's heart is again portrayed as hasty and misguided, emphasizing the "vast distances" between fleeting, superficial attractions and the enduring, deeper spiritual pursuit.

8. Blessed Moments

"Those blessed moments of closeness feel like a distant memory I miss.

Where are those flirtatious glances and reproaches now? Vast distances I find."

Hafez reminisces about past moments of closeness and intimacy, now feeling distant and unreachable. The "flirtatious glances and reproaches" symbolize the dynamic relationship with the divine, filled with both affection and chastisement. The "vast distances" highlight the poet's current sense of separation and longing for those spiritual highs.

9. Peace and Sleep

"Don't begrudge peace and sleep from Hafez, O friend!
Between peace, patience and sleep's embrace, vast distances I find."

In the final couplet, Hafez addresses a friend, asking not to be deprived of peace and sleep. He acknowledges the struggle between achieving peace, maintaining patience, and finding restful sleep, noting the "vast distances" between these states. This reflects the ongoing inner turmoil and yearning for tranquility.

This ghazal masterfully explores the contrasts and distances between various states of existence, from superficial piety to deep spiritual truth, from worldly beauty to divine grace, and from past joys to present longing. Each couplet stands as an independent unit, yet together they weave a tapestry of profound spiritual reflection and critique of societal norms. Through his eloquent use of imagery and metaphor, Hafez invites readers to ponder the vast distances in their own lives and seek a more genuine, heartfelt connection with the divine.

CHAPTER 16
GHAZAL 3 : BY LOVE'S COMMAND

اگر آن تُرک شیرازی به دست آرد دل ما را
به خال هِندویَش بخشم سمرقند و بخارا را

بده ساقی مِی باقی که در جنّت نخواهی یافت
کنار آب رُکن‌آباد و گلگشت مُصَلّا را

فَغان کاین لولیانِ شوخِ شیرینکارِ شهرآشوب
چنان بردند صبر از دل، که تُرکان خوان یغما را

. . .

ز عشقِ ناتمامِ ما جمالِ یار، مُستَغنی است
به آب و رنگ و خال و خط، چه حاجت روی زیبا را؟

من از آن حُسن روزافزون که یوسف داشت دانستم
که عشق از پردهٔ عصمت برون آرد زلیخا را

اگر دشنام فرمایی و گر نفرین، دعا گویم
جوابِ تلخ می‌زیبد، لبِ لعلِ شکرخا را

نصیحت گوش کن جانا، که از جان دوست‌تر دارند
جوانان سعادتمند پند پیر دانا را

حدیث از مطرب و مِی گو و رازِ دَهر کمتر جو
که کس نگشود و نگشاید به حکمت این معما را

غزل گفتی و دُر سفتی، بیا و خوش بخوان حافظ
که بر نظم تو افشاند فلک عِقد ثریّا را

GHAZAL 3 : BY LOVE'S COMMAND

Understand! Should that Turk of Shiraz seize our heart, through love's command
   Even for her dimple, I would readily trade Samarkand, by love's command.

Pour the wine, dear *Saghi*, for you'll never find even in heaven,
   Roknabad's little streams or *Mosalla's* fragrant roses, by love's command.

Alas! These mischievous, well-meaning *Luli* Sages who stir up the town
   Steal patience away like the Turks' battle cry to raid a land, by love's command.

Self-sufficient, Beloved's Beautiful Face, remains untouched by our unfulfilled love, for
   true beauty doesn't need makeup or embellishments, by love's command.

I knew from the grace of *Joseph's* growing beauty that love
   lured *Zuleikha* to breach the veil of modesty, by love's command.

No matter how you treat me: curse me or revile me, I still pray

for you; but does bitterness ever befit those sweet lips, by love's command?

My dear! Heed the words of the Sage, and so may you prosper

they are more valuable than life; hold on to them by love's command

So speak only of musicians, and of wine; seek less to unravel the mysteries of the universe.

For knowledge alone has, and will not, untie the mystery at hand, but only by love's command.

The ghazals you composed like pearls on necklace; come and recite them joyfully Hafez

For the heavens have applauded these pearly verses you cast as the necklace of the Pleiades, by love's command.

LULIAN: COMMENTARY ON TERMINOLOGY

The Term "ولیان" (Loulīān) in Hafez's Poetry

The term "ولیان" (Loulīān) holds significant meaning, particularly in the context of Sufi poetry. Historically, "Loulīān" refers to groups often perceived as marginalized or living on the fringes of society, such as vagabonds or gypsies. However, within the poetic and mystical traditions, they are more accurately likened to wandering dervishes or Sufis who are not confined to any single school or doctrine.

Symbolism of Loulīān

In Sufi poetry, the Loulīān symbolize free spirits who transcend societal norms and live according to their own rules. These individuals are often depicted as possessing esoteric knowledge and challenging the conventions of their time. This outsider status allows poets like Hafez to use them as metaphors for unorthodox approaches to mysticism, love, spirituality, and existence.

The path of the Loulīān mirrors that of the mystic: unbound by societal conventions, they seek a deeper, direct connection with the divine. Their practices and lifestyle, often seen as unconventional or even heretical by mainstream religious communities, highlight their commitment to a personal and profound spiritual journey.

Explanation of Specific Terms and Lines

فغان (Faghān): An exclamation expressing grief or sorrow, setting a tone of lamentation and emotional intensity.

لولیانِ شوخِ شیرین‌کارِ شهرآشوب (Mischievous, Sweet-Acting Rogues Who Stir Up the Town): These individuals, with their charm and allure, disrupt social norms. In Hafez's poetry, they symbolize beloveds whose beauty and charm unsettle the hearts of lovers, creating turmoil within the soul.

چنان بردند صبر از دل (Have Taken Away Patience from the Heart): Hafez expresses how these captivating individuals make it impossible for him to remain patient or calm, mirroring an infatuated lover's loss of peace due to the overwhelming presence of the beloved.

تُرکان خوان یغما را (As the Turks Call for Raids): Historically, this refers to invasions by Turkic tribes. Hafez uses this metaphor to emphasize the beloved's overwhelming and disruptive allure, comparing it to the unstoppable force of Turkic raids.

خوان یغما (Khān-e Yaghmā): Meaning "call for a raid," this phrase invokes memories of nomadic Turkic raids, symbolizing a powerful and sudden upheaval. It represents the intense and uncontrollable emotions stirred by the beloved's beauty..

Contextual Commentary on the Nature of Beauty

ز عشق ناتمامِ ما جمالِ یار، مُستَغنی است (The Beauty of the Beloved's Face is Self-sufficient, Untouched by Our Unfulfilled Love): This line suggests that the beauty of the beloved, often referring to the Divine in Sufi poetry, is independent of human love. The term "مستغنی" (mustaghna) means "self-sufficient" or "independent."

به آب و رنگ و خال و خط، چه حاجت روی زیبا را؟ (What Need Does a Truly Beautiful Face Have for Water, Color, Mole, and Line?): Hafez questions the need for superficial markers of beauty when true beauty is intrinsic and self-sufficient. This highlights the Sufi theme of valuing inner divine beauty over external appearances.

In this ghazal, Hafez masterfully intertwines themes of love, beauty, and spiritual wisdom, using rich imagery and cultural references to convey profound truths. Through his eloquent and layered use of language, Hafez invites readers to explore the depths of their own spiritual journeys, emphasizing the transformative power of love and the eternal quest for divine beauty. The analogy to Chinese sages underscores a universal quest for deeper truths that transcend cultural and historical boundaries.

Hafez's use of these terms and metaphors attempts to capture the profound impact of beauty and love on the human heart. By comparing the allure of the beloved to the formidable raids of nomadic tribes, he highlights the irresistible and often tumultuous nature of such emotions.

The Loulīān, with their free-spirited and unconventional ways, serve as perfect symbols for the mystic's path—one that defies societal norms in pursuit of a deeper, more authentic connection with the divine. Their presence in the poem *underscores the tension between societal expectations and the true desires of the heart*, reflecting the poet's own struggles and insights.

Readers are invited to contemplate deeply on the overwhelming power of love and beauty, urging us to recognize the profound and often disruptive force these elements can have on one's life and weigh the implications and ramifications. His use of layered language, offers a pause, a timeless contemplation on the nature of human longing contrasted with spiritual pursuit.

Loulian and Analogies to Chinese Sages

As discussed earlier, in classical Persian literature, particularly within the context of Sufi poetry, the term "ولیان" (Loulīān) refers to individuals who live on the margins of society. Historically, these groups were seen as vagabonds or gypsies, but in a more accurate cultural and mystical sense, they are akin to wandering dervishes or Sufis who transcend traditional societal norms. The Loulīān are symbolic of free spirits, unconstrained by societal conventions, and are often celebrated for their esoteric knowledge and unorthodox approaches to mysticism, love, spirituality, and existence.

Symbolism of Loulīān

The Loulīān challenge societal conventions and live according to their own rules. Their somewhat marginalized status allows poets *to use them as symbols for deeper, more authentic spiritual pursuits*. These figures embody the path of the mystic: they seek a direct connection with the divine, often employing unconventional methods and generally tend to reject the superficiality of societal norms.

Analogies to Chinese Sages: Lao Tzu and Lieh Tzu

Drawing an analogy between the Persian Loulīān and the Chinese sages, Lao Tzu and Lieh Tzu, we find possible shared themes in their relationship to societal norms and their emphasis on a deeper understanding of the universe's underlying truths.

Lao Tzu:

- **Philosophy:** Lao Tzu, the foundational figure of Taoism, is credited with writing the "Tao Te Ching," which explores the philosophy of the "Way" (Tao) and its virtues.
- **Wu Wei:** He emphasizes "wu wei" or "non-action," or "non-striving" suggesting that great power lies in not resisting the forces that shape Nature, the Dao and allowing nature or the Way, the Dao to take its course. "Keep to the center and let all things take their course" he suggests. *This concept seems to challenge common societal norms of striving and forcing outcomes.*
- *In the Tao Te Ching, Verse 29, Lao Tzu reminds us "Do you want to improve the world? I don't think it can be done. The world is sacred. It can't be improved. If you tamper with it, you'll ruin it. If you treat it like an object, you'll lose it." This verse emphasizes the importance of non-action and letting things take their course while we observe with intention.*
- **Simplicity and Humility:** Lao Tzu champions simplicity, humility, and living in harmony with the Tao, aligning with the Loulīān's rejection of societal conventions in favor of deeper spiritual truths.

Lieh Tzu:

- **Philosophy:** Lieh Tzu is another important Taoist philosopher known for his text "The Book of Master Lie," which emphasizes Taoist ideals through anecdotes and tales.
- **Living in Harmony:** Much like Lao Tzu, Lieh Tzu stresses living in harmony with nature and the cosmos, presenting

characters who may appear eccentric or non-conformist but possess deep wisdom.

Loulīan:

- **Free Spirits:** The Loulīan are celebrated in Persian culture for living on the margins of society, challenging conventions, and often embodying free spirits or mystics.
- **Unconventional Methods:** Like the Taoist sages, the Loulīan seek direct connections with the divine, using methods that are often seen as unorthodox, meditative techniques and conforming with the flow of Nature or Divine Will.

Pragmatic Conformity

Both in Taoist tradition and the symbolic usage of "ولیان" (Loulīan) in Persian literature, there is an understanding that *while these figures internally reject societal conventions, they often maintain an external appearance of conformity to protect themselves or to live harmoniously within society and not cause even greater disruptions by attempting to directly force change, but do so with subtler more indirect means of effecting change*.

Taoist Sages (Lao Tzu and Lieh Tzu):

- **Wu Wei:** The concept of "wu wei" in Taoism does not necessarily mean literal inaction but rather denotes action that aligns with the natural flow and avoids unnecessary disruption.
- **Navigating Society:** Taoist sages understand the perils of openly challenging societal norms. They might externally conform while internally adhering to their own understanding of the Tao, avoiding conflict and moving harmoniously within the societal structure.

Loulīan:

- **Dual Life:** The Loulīān, while celebrated for their free-spirited ways, often had to navigate societal expectations. In historical contexts, they might present a facade of conformity while practicing their unique meditations, practices and insights in private.
- **Poetic Hints:** Persian poetry often hints at this duality, showing the internal world of spiritual ecstasy alongside the external roles required by society. The Loulīān maintain an outward appearance of conformity to avoid backlash or persecution or creating chaos in society.

COMMENTARY

Let's explore each couplet in detail.

1. The Turk of Shiraz

"Understand! Should that Turk of Shiraz seize our heart, through love's command Even for her dimple, I would readily trade Samarkand, by love's command."

Hafez starts with an extravagant declaration of love, offering the cities of Samarkand and Bukhara for a mere dimple of his beloved, a "Turk of Shiraz." This hyperbolic statement highlights the poet's adoration and willingness to sacrifice immense worldly wealth for the beloved. The reference to the "Turk" and "Shiraz" ties into the cultural and historical context of Persian poetry, where Turks often symbolize beauty and Shiraz represents the poet's homeland.

2. Roknabad and Mosalla

"Pour the wine, dear Saghi, for you'll never find in any land, Roknabad's little streams or Mosalla's fragrant roses, by love's command."

Hafez invokes the imagery of Roknabad's streams and Mosalla's roses, places in Shiraz renowned for their beauty. He tells the Saghi (wine-bearer) to pour the wine, as such beauty cannot be found elsewhere, underscoring the uniqueness and irreplaceability of his beloved's charms. The wine represents divine love and spiritual intoxication, a recurring motif in Hafez's poetry.

3. Mischievous Sages

"Alas! These mischievous, sweet-acting Luli Sages[1] who stir up the town Steal patience away like the Turks' battle cry to raid a land, by love's command."

Hafez laments the disruptive yet charming influence of the Luli Sages, comparing their effect to the Turks' fearsome battle cries. This metaphor illustrates how the beauty and allure of these figures can destabilize one's peace and patience, much like an invading force. It emphasizes the overpowering nature of love and attraction.

4. Beauty's Self-Sufficiency

"The Beauty of the Beloved's Face is Self-sufficient, untouched by our unfulfilled love, True beauty doesn't need makeup or embellishments, by love's command."

In this couplet, Hafez declares that true beauty is self-sufficient and does not require adornment. The beloved's beauty stands apart from the poet's love, unaltered by his feelings. This highlights the concept of inner beauty and spiritual purity that transcends physical embellishments, a key theme in Sufi poetry.

5. Joseph and Zuleikha

"Joseph's beauty was so captivating, it grew with each passing day. Thus Zuleikha was lured to breach the veil of modesty, by love's command."

Hafez references the Biblical and Quranic story of Joseph and Zuleikha. Joseph's increasing beauty caused Zuleikha to abandon her modesty. This couplet explores the power of divine beauty to transcend and transform, leading individuals to acts they might not otherwise contemplate. It also alludes to the spiritual journey where divine love compels one to shed societal constraints.

6. Responding to the Beloved

"No matter how the beloved treats me: curse me or revile me, in disdain I will still respond with kindness and prayer, profound devotion, by love's command."

Hafez expresses unwavering devotion to the beloved, regardless of how he is treated. This reflects the Sufi ideal of selfless love and submission to the divine will. By responding to harsh treatment with

---

1. See section on Lulian.

kindness and prayer,Hafez illustrates the transformative power of love and spiritual resilience.

7. The Sage's Wisdom

"My dear! Heed the words of the Sage, and so may you prosper Hold them more valuable than life itself, in your hand, by love's command."

Hafez advises valuing the wisdom of the Sage, equating it to a treasure more precious than life. This couplet emphasizes the importance of spiritual guidance and the profound impact it can have on one's journey. The Sage symbolizes the enlightened teacher who leads seekers towards truth.

8. Musicians and Wine

"Speak of musicians and of wine; seek less of the mysteries of the universe. For knowledge alone has, and will not untie the mystery at hand, by love's command."

Hafez suggests focusing on the joys of music and wine instead of delving into the unfathomable mysteries of the universe. He implies that intellectual pursuits alone cannot solve life's deeper spiritual enigmas. This couplet underscores the Sufi belief in experiencing life's beauty and divine love directly rather than through mere contemplation.

9.Hafez's Ghazal

"Hafez come sing: you have composed a ghazal and strung pearls fast Stars applaud the verses you cast as the necklace of the Pleiades, by love's command."

In the final couplet, Hafez celebrates his own poetic creation, likening his verses to pearls strung into a necklace as beautiful as the Pleiades constellation. This self-referential couplet highlights his poetic prowess and the celestial quality of his ghazals. It serves as a triumphant conclusion, affirming the divine inspiration behind his art.

CHAPTER 17
GHAZAL 4: THE WORDS THAT BRING US TO DANCE

صبا به لطف بگو آن غزال رعنا را
که سر به کوه و بیابان تو داده‌ای ما را

شکرفروش که عمرش دراز باد چرا
تَفَقُّدی نکند طوطی شکرخا را

غرور حُسنت اجازت مگر نداد ای گل؟
که پرسشی نکنی عَندَلیب شیدا را

. . .

به خُلق و لطف توان کرد صید اهل نظر

به بند و دام نگیرند مرغ دانا را

ندانم از چه سبب رنگ آشنایی نیست

سَهی قدانِ سیَه چشمِ ماه سیما را

چو با حبیب نشینی و باده پیمایی

به یاد دار مُحِبّانِ بادپیما را

جز این قَدَر نتوان گفت در جمال تو عیب

که وضع مِهر و وفا نیست روی زیبا را

در آسمان نه عجب گر به گفتهٔ حافظ

سرود زُهره به رقص آورد مسیحا را

GHAZAL 4: THE WORDS THAT BRING US TO DANCE

O Morning Breeze, in gentle whisper, tell my Beloved, in words that bring us to dance
    you've made me flee to mountains and vast deserts, with the words that bring us to dance.

O Seller of sweets – may you live long! Would you not cast a graceful glance
    on this lowly parrot, so it too can fly with the words that bring us to dance?

Has beauty's pride not given you a chance, O radiant flower, to ask
    about the nightingale, so madly in love, so it sings the words that bring us to dance?

Through charm and grace, we can capture the attention of the Seer Sages,
    Not by traps or snares, can the wise bird be caught, but with words that bring us to dance.

I don't know why they make believe they don't know us; there's no mood of intimacy anymore –

those tall, moon-faced, black-eyed beauties, whose words bring us to dance.

When you sit with the Beloved, drinking in glee, remember us, passionate lovers
  deprived of the Beloved's presence, but with words that bring us to dance.

No other fault can be found in our radiant Beloved's otherwise impeccable beauty
  For such a face brings loyalty, genuine love and the words that bring us to dance.

In the vast expanse of the heavens, it's no wonder if, by these words, Hafez
  The melody of Venus brings the Messiah to glee, in a song that brings us to dance.

AHLE-NAZAR: COMMENTARY

Expanded Explanation of "اهل نظر" (Ahl-e-Nazar) in Mystical Persian Poetry

In the realm of mystical Persian poetry, vision metaphors are frequently used to describe spiritual experiences. Poets like Rumi, Hafez, and Attar often employ the act of seeing as a symbol for realization and enlightenment. The term "اهل نظر" (Ahl-e-Nazar) refers to the enlightened souls, mystics, and sages who have gained direct vision of the Ultimate Truth.

Detailed Understanding of the Seers: "اهل نظر" (Ahl-e-Nazar)

Literal Translation and Basic Meaning:

- اهل **(Ahl):** People of, possessors of, those who belong .
- نظر **(Nazar):** Sight, vision, gaze.

At a surface level, "اهل نظر" translates to "people of sight" or "those who possess vision" or the Seers, as in Seers of Reality; eg Sages. However, its implications run much deeper in a Sufi or mystical context.

Spiritual Vision: In Sufism, sight or vision is not limited to physical seeing. It often refers to inner vision, insight, or spiritual perception. Thus, "اهل نظر" denotes individuals who possess this inner sight or spiritual insight. These are people who see beyond the material world and grasp the deeper, spiritual realities of existence.

Intuitive Knowledge: Sufi tradition places great value on intuitive knowledge or direct cognition of the Divine. "اهل نظر" are those who have transcended mere intellectual understanding to achieve a direct, experiential knowledge of the Divine.

Recognition of Signs: In Sufi thought, everything in creation is considered a sign (آية) pointing to the Divine. "اهل نظر" are those who can read these signs, discerning the hidden messages in the universe around them.

Deep Discernment: In the face of life's ambiguities, "اهل نظر" have the capacity to discern truth from falsehood, reality from illusion. They have the sight to see through the veils that cloud most people's perceptions.

ANALOGIES TO CHINESE SAGES: LAO TZU AND LIEH TZU

Drawing an analogy between the Persian "اهل نظر" and the Chinese sages, Lao Tzu and Lieh Tzu, reveals shared themes in their relationship to societal norms and their emphasis on a deeper understanding of the universe's underlying truths.

Lao Tzu:

- **Philosophy:** Lao Tzu, the foundational figure of Taoism, is credited with writing the "Tao Te Ching," which explores the philosophy of the "Way" (Tao) and its virtues.
- **Wu Wei:** He emphasizes "wu wei" or "non-action," suggesting that great power lies in passivity and allowing nature or the Tao to take its course. This concept challenges societal norms of striving and forcing outcomes.
- **Simplicity and Humility:** Lao Tzu champions simplicity, humility, and living in harmony with the Tao, aligning with the "اهل نظر" rejection of societal conventions in favor of deeper spiritual truths.

Lieh Tzu:

- **Philosophy:** Lieh Tzu is another important Taoist philosopher known for his text "The Book of Master Lie," which emphasizes Taoist ideals through anecdotes and tales.
- **Living in Harmony:** Much like Lao Tzu, Lieh Tzu stresses living in harmony with nature and the cosmos, presenting characters who may appear eccentric or non-conformist but possess deep wisdom.

اهل نظر (Ahl-e-Nazar):

- **Free Spirits:** "اهل نظر" are celebrated in Persian culture for living on the margins of society, challenging conventions, and often embodying free spirits or mystics.
- **Unconventional Methods:** Like the Taoist sages, "اهل نظر" seek direct connections with the divine, using methods that are often seen as unorthodox.

Pragmatic Conformity

Both in Taoist tradition and the symbolic usage of "اهل نظر" in Persian literature, there is an understanding that while these figures internally reject societal conventions, they often maintain an external appearance of conformity to protect themselves or to live harmoniously within society.

Taoist Sages (Lao Tzu and Lieh Tzu):

- **Wu Wei:** The concept of "wu wei" in Taoism does not necessarily mean literal inaction but rather denotes action that aligns with the natural flow and avoids unnecessary disruption.
- **Navigating Society:** Taoist sages understand the perils of openly challenging societal norms. They might externally conform while internally adhering to their own understanding of the Tao, avoiding conflict and moving harmoniously within the societal structure.

اهل نظر (Ahl-e-Nazar):

- **Dual Life:** "اهل نظر," while celebrated for their free-spirited ways, often had to navigate societal expectations. In historical contexts, they might present a facade of conformity while practicing their unique rituals and insights in private.
- **Poetic Hints:** Persian poetry often hints at this duality, showing the internal world of spiritual ecstasy alongside the external roles required by society. "اهل نظر" maintain an outward appearance of conformity to avoid backlash or persecution.

POETIC EXPRESSION OF 'VISION'

Mystical Persian poets, like Rumi, Hafez, and Attar, often use vision metaphors to describe spiritual experiences. The act of seeing is symbolic of realization and enlightenment. "اهل نظر" in their verses refers to enlightened souls, mystics, and sages who have gained direct vision of the Ultimate Truth.

Inner Sight: In Sufism, sight or vision isn't restricted to physical seeing. It often refers to inner vision, insight, or spiritual perception. Thus, "اهل نظر" refers to individuals who possess inner sight or spiritual insight. These are people who see beyond the surface, beyond the material, and grasp the deeper, spiritual realities of existence.

Intuitive Knowledge: Sufi tradition places great value on intuitive knowledge or direct cognition of the Divine. "اهل نظر" are those who have moved beyond mere intellectual understanding to a direct, experiential knowledge of the Divine.

Recognition of Signs: Everything in creation is considered a sign (آية) pointing to the Divine. "اهل نظر" are those who can read these signs, discerning the hidden messages in the universe around them.

Deep Discernment: In the face of life's ambiguities, "اهل نظر" have the capacity to discern truth from falsehood, reality from illusion. They have the sight to see through the veils that cloud most people's perceptions.

Ghazal 4 as a Whole

The ghazal touches upon several profound Sufi concepts. Let's try to unravel some of these key concepts.

صبا به لطف بگو آن غزال رعنا را: Saba represents the divine wind or messenger, often evoked in Sufi poetry to convey messages. The "graceful gazelle" symbolizes the beloved, often a stand-in for the Divine or Truth in Sufi poetry. Asking the wind to convey a message emphasizes the seeker's longing and detachment from the material world.

شکرفروش که عمرش دراز باد چرا: Selling sugar (symbolizing spiritual sweetness and knowledge) is a metaphor for spiritual teaching. The parrot's longing for this sweetness indicates the soul's desire for divine knowledge.

غرور حُسنت اجازت مگر نداد ای گل؟: Here, Hafez touches on the concept of divine beauty and pride. The nightingale is traditionally symbolic of the lover or seeker, and the rose of the Divine or the beloved. Hafez is highlighting that overwhelming beauty can sometimes hinder true understanding or communication.

به خُلق و لطف توان کرد صید اهل نظر: The qualities of character and grace are emphasized as tools for "capturing" the attention or heart of the wise. This underlines the Sufi idea that inward qualities are more important than external rituals.

ندانم از چه سبب رنگ آشنایی نیست: Hafez speaks of the mystery of unfamiliarity, highlighting the journey of the seeker who feels distant from the Divine despite being close.

چو با حبیب نشینی و باده پیمایی: Sitting with the beloved and drinking wine are classical metaphors for spiritual union and intoxication with the divine love. Remembering others signifies the selflessness and consciousness of a true lover.

جز این قَدَر نتوان گفت در جمال تو عیب: Here, Hafez speaks of the incomparable beauty of the beloved (Divine), so pure that even loyalty and love don't do justice to it.

در آسمان نه عجب گر به گفتهٔ حافظ: This verse encapsulates the transcendental power of true poetry. Venus (Zohreh) symbolizes beauty and allure, while Messiah (Jesus) is associated with spirituality and salvation. The idea is that true poetry or words of wisdom can move even the highest spiritual beings.

The Sentiment of Remembrance

The couplet beautifully portrays a sentiment common in Persian mystical poetry: the act of wine-drinking as a metaphor for spiritual intoxication or divine love. When you are in the company of the "beloved" (which can mean a physical beloved or the Divine) and partake in this "wine" (divine love or spiritual experience), remember those lovers who have similarly been intoxicated by this experience. Hafez urges remembrance, implying a sense of unity or solidarity among all those who have tread the path of love.

In many traditional settings, particularly in the context of Sufi gatherings or mystic poetical sessions, remembering those who aren't present (physically or metaphorically) is a common theme. The "wine-drinking" can be both a literal and metaphorical experience. Literally, it refers to enjoying wine in a gathering, and metaphorically, it alludes to the intoxication of divine love or spiritual enlightenment.

When Hafez mentions "Remember the wine-drinking lovers," he could be alluding to:

- **Those Physically Absent:** Friends or fellow seekers who couldn't attend the gathering for some reason.
- **Those Spiritually Seeking:** Individuals who are yearning for the same intoxicating experience of divine love but haven't yet reached that state.
- **Past Lovers/Mystics:** Remembering the great lovers or Sufi mystics of the past, acknowledging their experiences and seeking inspiration from them.

The sentiment of remembrance brings forth a sense of communal unity and continuity in the experience of mystical love and spiritual longing, acknowledging both those who partake in the present moment and those who, for whatever reason, cannot join us.

So, "اهل نظر" (Ahle-nazar) represents not just those with physical sight but those who possess spiritual vision and discernment, capable of recognizing the deeper realities of existence and the Divine. They embody the pinnacle of spiritual evolution in the Sufi path, having transcended mere intellectual knowledge to achieve direct cognition of the Ultimate.

CHAPTER 18
GHAZAL 5: HELP ME FOR I AM ABOUT TO REVEAL SECRETS

دل می‌رود ز دستم صاحب‌دلان خدا را
دردا که راز پنهان خواهد شد آشکارا

کشتی‌شکستگانیم ای باد شُرطِه برخیز
باشد که باز بینم دیدار آشنا را

دمروزه مِهر گردون، افسانه است و افسون
نیکی به جای یاران فرصت شمار یارا

در حلقهٔ گل و مُل خوش خواند دوش بلبل

هاتِ الصَّبُوحَ هُبّوا یا ایُّها السُکارا

ای صاحب کرامت شکرانهٔ سلامت
روزی تَفَقُّدی کن درویش بی‌نوا را

آسایش دو گیتی تفسیر این دو حرف است
با دوستان مروت با دشمنان مدارا

در کوی نیکنامی ما را گذر ندادند
گر تو نمی‌پسندی تغییر کن قضا را

آن تلخ‌وَش که صوفی اُمّ‌الخَبائِثَش خواند
اَشهی لَنا و اَحلی مِن قُبلَةِ العَذارا

هنگام تنگدستی در عیش کوش و مستی
کاین کیمیای هستی قارون کُنَد گدا را

سرکش مشو که چون شمع از غیرتت بسوزد
دلبر که در کف او موم است سنگ خارا

آیینهٔ سکندر، جام می است بنگر
تا بر تو عرضه دارد احوال مُلک دارا

خوبان پارسی‌گو، بخشندگان عمرند
ساقی بده بشارت رندان پارسا را

حافظ به خود نپوشید این خرقهٔ می‌آلود

ای شیخ پاکدامن معذور دار ما را

GHAZAL 5: HELP ME FOR I AM ABOUT TO REVEAL SECRETS

HELP ME FRIENDS, my heart is slipping from my grasp, on the verge of revealing, with these overwhelming feelings
It would pain me, if these secrets were revealed, because of these overwhelming feelings

We the shipwrecked, hope to see the face of friends, even once more
as storms assail, amid the fierce gale, they rise, these overwhelming feelings

The short lived love of this world is a fleeting tale, an enchantment,
Choose kindness, my friend, for the time with friends is limited despite these overwhelming feelings

In the circle of roses and jasmine, the nightingale sang sweetly last night,
'Rise and bring the morning drink, O you, who feel these overwhelming feelings'

. . .

O Possessor of Grace, we pray gratefully for your well-being, today, look upon us

destitute followers (dervishes) who are overrun with these overwhelming feelings.

Comfort & peace in both worlds, is but a commentary on these two points:

With friends– kindness and with foes– patience, despite these overwhelming feelings.

They did not let us through the streets of good reputation easily,

But if you don't approve, change fate with these overwhelming feelings

In times of hardship, seek inner joy and intoxication, because with alchemy of Existence,

you can transform a poverty to Treasures despite these overwhelming feelings

Know that in the hands of the Beloved, stone transforms to wax,

So don't be headstrong, for jealousy will burn you like a candle, in these overwhelming feelings

Did you know the mirror of Alexander is a cup of wine? Look – you can see the future

state of those who hold the realms of power, despite these overwhelming feelings.

Those sophisticated Persian-speaking Righteous ones, those bestowers of life,

With them share this news; with the Sages, O Saghi, using these overwhelming feelings

Hafez, did not himself choose to wear this wine-stained cloak,
    O purest of Masters, excuse us, amid these overwhelming feelings.

CHAPTER 19
DETAILED SUFI AND MYSTICAL COMMENTARY

1. The Slipping Heart

In Sufi poetry, the heart slipping from one's grasp often symbolizes the heart's journey towards divine love, which can feel overwhelming and uncontrollable. The "secrets" refer to the mystical experiences and inner states of the Sufi, which are typically hidden from the uninitiated. The fear of these secrets being revealed indicates the vulnerability and sanctity of these experiences and the concern they may fall in misguided hands and minds.

Hafez begins with an appeal to the enlightened souls (the "Dear Ones"), expressing the intense emotional turmoil that makes his heart feel like it's slipping from his control. He fears that his deep, hidden emotions and secrets will be exposed, emphasizing the vulnerability that comes with such profound feelings.

2. The Shipwrecked Seek Salvation

The metaphor of being shipwrecked reflects the spiritual seeker's state of loss and despair, seeking the "fair wind" of divine grace to guide them back to a state of spiritual union. Seeing the "face of friends" can symbolize the reunion with fellow seekers or with the Divine Beloved.

In this couplet, Hafez describes himself and others as shipwrecked souls, longing for a fair wind to rise and guide them to safety. This fair wind symbolizes hope and divine intervention that could reunite them with their beloved friends. The imagery of shipwreck highlights the sense of being lost and overwhelmed by emotions.

3. Fleeting Love

The short-lived love of the universe is a fleeting tale – an enchantment, Seize the moment, my friend, for time with friends is finite, choose kindness despite these overwhelming feelings.

This couplet emphasizes the impermanence of worldly love and pleasures. Sufi philosophy teaches that true love is eternal and divine, unlike the fleeting attachments of the material world. The call to seize the moment and display kindness to friends reflects the importance of spiritual companionship amid the transient nature of life.

Hafez reflects on the transient nature of worldly love, likening it to a fleeting tale or enchantment. He advises his friend to cherish the moments spent with loved ones, and show deep kindness (Niki) as time is limited. This couplet underscores the importance of valuing relationships despite the overwhelming emotions they may bring or we may have.

4. The Nightingale's Song

در حلقهٔ گل و مُل خوش خواند دوش بلبل هاتِ الصَّبُوحَ هُبّوا یا ایّها السُکارا

"In the circle of roses and jasmine, the nightingale sang sweetly last night, 'Arise and bring the morning drink, O you who feel these overwhelming feelings.'"

The nightingale's song is a common Sufi metaphor for the call of the Divine to the soul. The "morning drink" represents spiritual intoxication, a state of bliss or enlightenment. The roses and jasmine symbolize the beauty and richness of the divine presence, inviting the seeker to awaken to a higher state of consciousness.

Hafez evokes the imagery of a beautiful garden where the nightingale's song invites the listeners to rise and embrace the day with a morning drink. This scene symbolizes the celebration of life and the encouragement to find joy amidst overwhelming emotions, a joy that not only comes from searching outside but often from searching deep within and finding the very source of bliss within, through meditation. The nightingale's song represents the call to savor the present moment and transcend.

5. Grateful Dervishes

ای صاحب کرامت شکرانهٔ سلامت روزی تَفَقُّدی کن درویش بینوا را

"O possessor of grace, grateful are we, for your well-being. So today, look upon us, destitute followers (dervish: a spiritual seeker who has wilfully given up worldly possessions) who have these over-whelming feelings."

Here, Hafez expresses gratitude to the Divine or a spiritual master for their grace and well-being. The "destitute followers" or dervishes are those who have renounced worldly attachments in pursuit of spiri-tual wealth. This plea for attention is a humble request for divine favor and guidance.

Here we have an expression of gratitude to a gracious figure, likely a spiritual guide or the Divine. He asks for a moment of attention towards the destitute followers (dervishes) who are overwhelmed by their emotions. This plea highlights the humility and dependence on the benevolence of the spiritual guide.

6. Comfort in Both Worlds

آسایش دو گیتی تفسیر این دو حرف است با دوستان مروت با دشمنان مدارا

"Comfort in both worlds – a commentary on these two points: With friends – kindness, with foes – patience, despite these overwhelming feelings."

Sufi Perspective: This couplet distills the essence of Sufi ethics. True comfort in both the material and spiritual realms comes from showing kindness to friends and patience with enemies. These virtues are central to the Sufi way of life, promoting harmony and spiritual growth despite emotional challenges.

Hafez distills wisdom into two principles: showing kindness to friends and exercising patience with enemies. These virtues are presented as the path to achieving comfort in both the material and spiritual worlds, despite the emotional turmoil one may experience.

7. Changing Fate

در کوی نیکنامی ما را گذر ندادند گر تو نمی‌پسندی تغییر کن قضا را

"They did not allow us to pass through the streets of good repute, But if you don't approve, then transform fate with these overwhelming feelings."

Hafez speaks of being barred from the "streets of good repute," which could symbolize societal rejection or spiritual obstacles. The challenge to "transmute fate" suggests the Sufi belief in the transformative power of spiritual practice and inner resolve, even against predestined outcomes.

Being barred from the "streets of good repute." This suggests societal or reputational obstacles. He challenges the reader to change their fate if they do not approve of their current circumstances, emphasizing the power of emotions or the state of inner ecstasy, transcendance to drive transformation.

8. Inner Joy in Hardship

هنگام تنگدستی در عیش کوش و مستی کاین کیمیای هستی قارون کُنَد گدا را

"In times of hardship, seek inner joy and intoxication (euphoria, ecstasy, transcendence, spiritual bliss), For with the alchemy of Existence, you can transform a beggar to kingly status with treasured riches, [despite these overwhelming feelings.]"

This couplet advises finding joy and spiritual intoxication even during difficult times. The "alchemy of Existence" refers to the transformative power of divine love and spiritual insight, which can elevate the soul from poverty to spiritual wealth.

Hafez advises finding joy and euphoria even during hardship. He refers to the "alchemy of Existence," which has the power to transform a beggar into a person of great wealth. This metaphor speaks to the transformative potential of spiritual enlightenment and resilience.

9. Humility and Grace

سرکش مشو که چون شمع از غیرتت بسوزد دلبر که در کف او موم است سنگ خارا

"Know that in the beloved's hands, stone becomes wax, So do not be headstrong, for jealousy will burn you like a candle, with these overwhelming feelings."

Hafez warns against pride and jealousy, comparing them to a candle's flame that can consume you and cause destruction. The beloved's power to transform "stone to wax" symbolizes the transformative and softening influence of divine love on a hardened heart.

So, Hafez warns against stubbornness and jealousy, comparing them to a candle's flame that can burn. He emphasizes the transformative power of the beloved, who can soften even the hardest of hearts. The imagery of stone becoming wax under the beloved's touch symbolizes the malleability and transformation possible through love.

10. Alexander's Mirror

آیینهٔ سکندر، جام می است بنگر تا بر تو عرضه دارد احوال مُلک دارا

"Alexander's mirror is a cup of wine – but look! You can see the future of those – who hold the realms of power, despite these over-whelming feelings."

Comparing a cup of wine to Alexander's mirror, Hafez suggests that divine intoxication (symbolized by wine) provides insight into the future and the nature of power. This aligns with the Sufi idea that spiritual enlightenment reveals deeper truths about existence and destiny.

The phrase "آیینهٔ سکندر" (Aayineh-ye Sekandar) or "The Mirror of Alexander" is imbued with profound philosophical and mystical significance in Sufi thought, drawing upon the historical and mythical narratives of Alexander the Great (known as Sekandar in Persian liter-ature). This concept is explored through various layers of symbolism, each offering a unique spiritual lesson:

Divine Reflection

In Sufi mysticism, mirrors often symbolize the heart or the soul, which, when purified, reflect the divine truth. Rumi, for example, speaks of polishing the mirror, referring to inner meditation that polishes the dust or rust off of the inner mirror that reflects ourselves. Alexander's mirror, in this context, is seen as a metaphor for the human heart or consciousness (two levels of meaning) . The idea is that just as Alexander might use a mirror to view his physical surround-ings, the seeker uses the heart to perceive spiritual realities. This reflec-tion is not just of the self but of the divine light, emphasizing the unity of all existence under God's omnipresence.

Quest for Immortality

Historical and mythical tales sometimes depict Alexander the Great's quest for the Water of Life, a journey aimed at achieving immortality. In these stories, the mirror might serve as a tool or symbol guiding Alexander to this ultimate elixir. For Sufis, this narrative trans-forms into a metaphor for the spiritual quest for eternal life through enlightenment and union with the divine, rather than a physical pursuit. The mirror reflects the eternal truth and the illusory nature of temporal existence.

Self-Realization and Enlightenment

In a more introspective interpretation, the mirror represents the process of self-examination and recognition of one's inner divine nature. Alexander's journey with the mirror symbolizes the spiritual journey where the seeker confronts and overcomes personal limitations and illusions. This self-realization is critical in Sufism, which values the inner knowledge that leads to the recognition of one's soul as a reflection of God.

The World as a Mirror

Extending the metaphor further, Sufi philosophy often views the entire cosmos as a mirror reflecting the divine. In this sense, Alexander's mirror could symbolize the universe itself, with everything within it reflecting aspects of the divine nature. This understanding encourages a perception of the world that is imbued with spiritual significance, where every creature, object, and event is a sign of the divine presence.

Historical and Cultural Context

The story of Alexander and his mirror also intersects with various cultural and historical narratives within Persian literature, such as the "Shahnameh" and other epic poems, where Alexander is portrayed not only as a conqueror but also as a seeker of wisdom. This dual depiction enriches the Sufi interpretation of the mirror, adding layers of heroic quest and philosophical inquiry.

Each of these interpretations contributes to the rich tapestry of meanings associated with "The Mirror of Alexander" in Sufi thought, highlighting themes of divine reflection, the quest for immortality, self-realization, and the understanding of the world as a divine mirror. These themes are central to Sufi mysticism, which seeks to transcend the superficial aspects of life to reach deeper spiritual truths.

Hafez compares a cup of wine to Alexander's mirror, which is said to reveal the future. This suggests that through the intoxicating experience of divine love (symbolized by wine), one can gain profound insights into the future and the nature of power. It emphasizes the wisdom and foresight gained through spiritual intoxication.

11. Righteous Beings

خوبان پارسی‌گو، بخشندگان عمرند ساقی بده بشارت رندان پارسا را

"Those righteous Persian-speaking beings – those bestowers of life, share the news with those righteous sages, O saghi, despite these over-whelming feelings."

Hafez praises the righteous Persian-speaking individuals who are like bestowers of life, possibly referring to wise and enlightened beings. He asks the saghi (wine-bearer) to share the good news with these sages, emphasizing the communal and shared nature of spiritual wisdom.

The verse you've provided, "خوبان پارسی‌گو، بخشندگان عمرند ساقی بده" را پارسا رندان بشارت" (Khooban-e Parsi-gu, bakhshandegan-e omrand; Saqi bedeh besharat-e randan-e parsa ra), offers a rich tapestry of historical, cultural, and spiritual connotations, particularly within the context of Persian poetry and Sufi literature. This line can be translated as, "The beautiful Persian speakers, they are givers of life; O cupbearer, give good tidings to the pious libertines."

Historical and Cultural Context

Language and Expression: The term "خوبان پارسی‌گو" (beautiful Persian speakers) not only highlights physical beauty but also the beauty of the Persian language, known for its elegance and poetic rich-ness. Historically, Persian was the lingua franca of much of the Islamic world in medieval times, used in court and in literary works, and it carried a connotation of cultural and intellectual sophistication.

Cupbearer and Wine Imagery: The use of the term "ساقی" (Saqi, or cupbearer) and the reference to wine-serving is a common motif in Persian poetry, symbolizing divine grace and spiritual intoxication. The cupbearer, often a symbol of divine agency, serves wine that repre-sents knowledge and enlightenment, leading to a transcendent under-standing of the divine.

Spiritual Context

Givers of Life: The phrase "بخشندگان عمرند" (givers of life) metaphor-ically refers to those who impart wisdom and spiritual enlightenment, akin to giving 'life' to the soul. In Sufism, true life is considered the spiritual awakening and connection with the divine, beyond mere physical existence.

Pious Libertines: The reference to "رندان پارسا" (pious libertines) is particularly intriguing. In Persian Sufi poetry, 'Rind' often refers to a figure who appears outwardly libertine but is inwardly pious and free from worldly attachments. This archetype challenges conventional religious orthodoxy and suggests that true piety is a matter of the heart, not merely external adherence to norms.

Announcement of Good Tidings: The command "بده بشارت" (give good tidings) signifies the announcement of spiritual joy or enlightenment. This could be interpreted as a call to celebrate the inner spiritual liberation that comes from understanding and embracing the divine truth, as facilitated by the teachings and beauty of the Persian speakers and the spiritual wine served by the cupbearer.

Integration in Sufi Poetry

This verse encapsulates the essence of Sufi poetry's use of symbolic language to convey deep spiritual truths. Persian Sufi poets like Hafez, Rumi, and Saadi often utilized such imagery to express concepts of divine love, *the paradox of outward appearances versus inner realities, and the celebration of divine grace.* The verse serves as an invitation to perceive beyond the superficial and recognize the deeper spiritual messages conveyed through beauty, language, and symbolic acts like the serving of wine.

This line blends historical language pride, cultural motifs of beauty and revelry, and profound spiritual insights characteristic of Sufi mysticism, offering a multifaceted insight into the depths of Persian spiritual and cultural heritage.

Hafez speaks of the righteous beings who bestow life and wisdom. He asks the saghi (wine-bearer) to share the good news with these sages, highlighting the value of sharing spiritual insights and celebrating righteousness despite emotional challenges.

12. Hafez's Cloak

حافظ به خود نپوشید این خرقهٔ مِی‌آلود ای شیخ پاکدامن معذور دار ما را

"O Hafez, did not wilfully wear this wine-stained cloak, O purely-attired Master, please forgive us, amidst these overwhelming feelings."

Hafez addresses himself, acknowledging his reluctance to embrace worldly intoxication (symbolized by the wine-stained cloak). He appeals to a pure-hearted master for forgiveness, recognizing his own spiritual struggles and seeking grace.

Adding to the interpretation of the verse "حافظ به خود نپوشید این خرقهٔ می‌آلود ای شیخ پاکدامن معذور دار ما را", we can further contextualize it with the understanding that "Hafez has not willingly donned this wine-stained cloak; O pure-minded Sheikh, excuse us." Here, Hafez is emphasizing that his actions, including his metaphorical wearing of a wine-stained cloak, are not out of personal choice or desire but are driven by a divine decree or predestined path.

Expanded Commentary and Interpretation

Lack of Personal Choice: The additional interpretation suggests that Hafez views his actions as not being a result of his own volition ("به اختیار خود نپوشیده است"). This aligns with the Sufi belief in divine will and predestination, where every action and event is seen as part of a greater divine plan. By stating this, Hafez shifts the responsibility of his spiritual state from personal choice to divine will, challenging conventional judgments about piety and sin.

Divine Determinism: Hafez's assertion that his actions are "به حکم ازلی" (by eternal decree) introduces a philosophical stance on divine determinism, where every aspect of one's life, including their faults and virtues, are orchestrated by divine will. This perspective invites a reevaluation of moral and spiritual accountability, suggesting that human beings are players in a divinely scripted play, with their roles and actions determined by a higher power.

Appeal for Understanding: By asking the Sheikh (master, spiritual guide) to "excuse us" (معذور بدار), Hafez is not just seeking forgiveness for himself but also advocating for a broader understanding and compassion towards all individuals who may seem to deviate from religious norms. It's an appeal to the Sheikh to recognize the complex dynamics of divine will in human actions and to judge less harshly.

Critique of Superficial Judgments: This interpretation further deepens the critique of outward religious appearances and judgments. Hafez challenges the Sheikh, and by extension the religious establishment, to look beyond the surface and consider the deeper, often hidden, motivations and circumstances that shape human behavior.

This critique is a call for a more profound, nuanced, and empathetic approach to spirituality and human imperfection.

Integration in Sufi Philosophy

In the broader Sufi philosophy, this verse and its interpretations highlight the mystic's journey towards understanding and aligning with the divine will, recognizing the limitations of human judgment and the profundity of divine wisdom. Hafez, through his poetry, often explores these themes, using personal anecdotes and symbolic imagery to discuss the nature of fate, the illusion of free will, and the pursuit of true understanding and compassion.

In the final couplet, Hafez addresses himself, acknowledging his refusal to don the wine-stained cloak, a symbol of worldly intoxication and imperfection. He appeals to a purely-attired Master (possibly a spiritual guide or the Divine) for forgiveness, recognizing his own shortcomings and seeking grace amidst his overwhelming feelings.

The imagery of the heart, shipwreck, fleeting love, nightingale, and transformation all serve to illustrate the soul's journey towards divine love and enlightenment. Remember that in the Ghazal structure, each couplet tends to add a layer of meaning, emphasizing the transformative power of spiritual practices, the importance of kindness and patience, and the ultimate quest for divine union amidst overwhelming feelings.

CHAPTER 20
GHAZAL 6: WHO WILL PASS ON THIS PRAYER?

به ملازمان سلطان که رساند این دعا را؟
که به شُکرِ پادشاهی ز نظر مران گدا را

ز رقیب دیوسیرت به خدای خود پناهم
مگر آن شهاب ثاقب مددی دهد خدا را

مژهٔ سیاهت ار کرد به خون ما اشارت
ز فریب او بیندیش و غلط مکن نگارا

دل عالمی بسوزی چو عِذار برفُروزی

تو از این چه سود داری که نمی‌کنی مدارا

همه شب در این امیدم که نسیم صبحگاهی
به پیام آشنایان بنوازد آشنا را

چه قیامت است جانا که به عاشقان نمودی؟
دل و جان فدای رویت بنما عِذار ما را

به خدا که جرعه‌ای ده تو به حافظ سحرخیز
که دعای صبحگاهی اثری کند شما را

GHAZAL 6: WHO WILL PASS ON THIS PRAYER?

To the king's aides, who will pass on this prayer?
    May you be healthy! May you not spurn beggars with your gaze, is
our prayer

From the evil-natured rival, I seek refuge in the Almighty God,
    Perhaps the meteor that struck the enemy, came to lend aid from
the Lord with this prayer

If your dark eyelashes may want to signal our blood,
    Beware the rival's deceit and do not err, my beloved, listen to this
prayer

You set the heart of the world ablaze, as you inflame everything with
charm,
    What benefit is it to you if you show no grace or regard? Hear this
prayer!

All night, I hope the morning breeze, draws near, and will caress
    dear ones with loving messages born from this prayer.

Our Beloved! What overwhelming alchemy you have shown lovers!
     May heart and soul be sacrificed for you, to cover our flaws, with this prayer.

For God's sake, gift a single sip to Hafez, the dawn-riser.
     May it bear fruit and grant us your attention, this morning prayer.

CHAPTER 21
COMMENTARY ON GHAZAL 6

DETAILED COMMENTARY on Hafez's Ghazal

This ghazal by Hafez explores themes of divine love, spiritual long-ing, and the transient nature of life, using vivid metaphors and intri-cate imagery. Each couplet reveals different aspects of the poet's emotional and spiritual journey, intertwined with a plea for mercy and grace. Here is a detailed commentary on each couplet, with a focus on Sufi and mystical interpretations.

1. The King's Aides

"To the king's aides, who will pass on this prayer? Keep healthy! May you not spurn beggars with your gaze, is this prayer."

Hafez begins by addressing the aides of the king, asking who will convey his prayer. He wishes them health and urges them not to dismiss beggars. This plea for compassion and humility from those in power reflects a deeper spiritual request for divine mercy and grace, emphasizing the Sufi values of humility and kindness.

2. Seeking Refuge from Rivals

"From the evil-natured rival, I seek refuge in my God, Perhaps that striking meteor came to lend aid from the Lord with this prayer."

He seeks refuge from a malicious rival, placing his trust in God. The striking meteor symbolizes divine intervention and protection. This couplet highlights the Sufi belief in relying on divine support during adversities, portraying the struggle against both inner and outer enemies.

3. The Beloved's Dark Eyelashes

"If your dark eyelashes may want to signal our blood, Beware the rival's deceit and do not err, my beloved, listen to this prayer."

Hafez warns his beloved to be cautious of the rival's deceit. The dark eyelashes represent the allure and potential danger of the beloved's beauty. This couplet underscores the complexity of love and the need for vigilance against deceit, reflecting the Sufi idea of the beloved's beauty being both a source of attraction and a test for the lover.

4. The World's Heart Ablaze

"You set the world's heart ablaze, as you inflame everything with charm, What benefit is it to you if you show no grace or regard, with this prayer?"

He praises the beloved's charm, which ignites the world's heart, but questions the benefit of not showing grace. This couplet highlights the paradox of the beloved's beauty causing both joy and suffering. In Sufi thought, it reflects on the divine beauty that attracts and tests the seeker, emphasizing the need for grace and compassion.

5. The Morning Breeze

"All night, in hopes that the morning breeze, so near, Will caress loved ones with loving messages born from this prayer."

Hafez expresses hope that the morning breeze will carry loving messages to his beloved. The morning breeze symbolizes divine grace and spiritual messages. This couplet reflects the Sufi practice of night vigils and the hope for divine communication and blessings.

6. Overwhelming Transformation

"What overwhelming transformation, beloved, you have shown lovers! May heart and soul be sacrificed for your face (Seeing you) ; and may you pay us attention, with this prayer."

He marvels at the profound impact the beloved has on lovers, describing it as an overwhelming transformation. He offers his heart and soul in devotion, asking the beloved to provide their attention to the poet. This couplet speaks to the transformative power of divine love, initiated through the unbending intent of the seeker, their prayer and attention to draw the attention of the beloved, the Divine. This relates to the Sufi quest for self-awareness and purification.

7. The Morning Prayer

"For God's sake, give (gift, grant) a sip to Hafez, the dawn riser, May it bring results for you, with this morning prayer."

In the final couplet, Hafez asks for a sip of wine, symbolizing divine grace, as he rises at dawn for prayer. He believes that this morning prayer will bring blessings to the giver. This reflects the Sufi practice of early morning devotions and the belief in the power of sincere prayer to bring divine favor.

This intricately weaves themes of divine love, human longing, and spiritual transformation.

CHAPTER 22
GHAZAL 7: GAZE INTO THE POLISHED MIRROR

صوفی بیا که آینه صافیست جام را
تا بنگری صفای می لعل‌فام را

راز درون پرده ز رندان مست پرس
کاین حال نیست زاهد عالی‌مقام را

عَنقا شکار کَس نشود دام بازچین
کانجا همیشه باد به دست است، دام را

در بزم دور، یک‌دو قدح درکش و برو

یعنی طمع مدار وصال دوام را

ای دل شباب رفت و نچیدی گلی ز عیش
پیرانه‌سر مکن هنری ننگ و نام را

در عیش نقد کوش که چون آبخور نماند
آدمْ بهشتْ، روضهٔ دارُالسَلام را

ما را بر آستان تو بس حق خدمت است
ای خواجه بازبین به تَرَحُّم غلام را

حافظ مرید جام می است ای صبا برو
وز بنده بندگی برسان شیخ جام را

GHAZAL 7: GAZE INTO THE POLISHED MIRROR

Come Sufi, gaze into the polished mirror of the cup, *beyond the veil of secrets*,
    To see the clarity of the ruby-red wine, beyond the veil of secrets,

The so-called high-ranked pious have not accessed this inner state.
    Ask the drunken Rend to reveal what goes on beyond the veil of secrets

The Phoenix eludes capture, ever soaring beyond snares and worldly schemes,
    For the wind frees the net every time, teaching us — beyond the veil of secrets,

In life's fleeting feast, sip once or twice, then vanish like the evening mist,
    Understand, the permanence of union is not to be grasped, beyond the veil of secrets,

Oh heart, youth has slipped away, with too few roses plucked from life's garden,

Don't grow old with honor untested; a faded crest beyond the veil of secrets,

Pursue the bliss in this moment, for like water in the hand, it slips through the fingers,
Adam left paradise, a tale whispered softly beyond the veil of secrets,

Coming to your threshold for service is enough for us, our hands worn, but hearts hopeful,
Master, look kindly upon us, the humbled, once more, as you gaze beyond the veil of secrets,

Hafez, devotee of the cup, seeks the wine's whisper but speaks not of what he hears,
And bids the morning breeze to carry a disciple's fealty to the aster, beyond the veil of secrets.

Oh Morning breeze, carry this message: Hafez is a devotee of the wine cup,
to the Master of the cup, that he is your devotee, beyond the veil of secrets.

COMMENTARY

Sufi Reflection: The Mirror of the Cup

In the first couplet, "صوفی" (Sufi), Hafez invites the Sufi, a mystic devoted to experiencing the divine, to gaze into the polished mirror of the cup. This symbolizes self-reflection and inner purity. The ruby-red wine within represents divine love and mystical knowledge, visible only when one transcends worldly illusions.

The Zahid and the Rend: Contrasting Piety with Spiritual Intoxication

In the second couplet, "زاهد" (Zahid), Hafez contrasts the outwardly pious with true mystics, who possess profound spiritual experiences. The high-ranked pious, who have not accessed this inner state, ask the drunken Rend, a spiritually intoxicated dervish, to reveal the secrets of divine love and knowledge.

The Phoenix: Symbol of Spiritual Rebirth and Immortality

In the third couplet, "عَنقا" (Phoenix), Hafez uses the Phoenix, a symbol of immortality and spiritual rebirth, to illustrate that the soul cannot be trapped by materialistic desires. Divine grace, likened to the wind, ensures the soul's spiritual freedom, freeing it from worldly snares.

Life's Fleeting Feast: Embracing Transient Moments

In the fourth couplet, "در بزم دور" (life's fleeting feast), Hafez advises enjoying life's fleeting moments without attachment, comparing life to a feast where one should sip the wine of joy before vanishing like the evening mist. This highlights the transient nature of experiences and the impermanence of spiritual union in this world.

Youth: The Garden of Opportunities

In the fifth couplet, "شباب" (youth), Hafez reflects on the missed opportunities of youth, urging not to grow old without having tested one's honor and achievements. He uses the metaphor of plucking roses from life's garden to symbolize moments of joy and meaningful experiences.

Present Bliss: The Ephemeral Nature of Happiness

In the sixth couplet, "عیش نقد" (present bliss), Hafez emphasizes living in the present and cherishing fleeting moments of happiness. He compares these moments to water slipping through fingers, underscoring their ephemeral nature. The story of Adam leaving paradise illustrates the transient nature of bliss.

Devotion in Service: Seeking Compassion at the Divine Threshold

In the seventh couplet, "خدمت" (service), Hafez speaks of the devotion of seekers who come to serve at the divine threshold, describing their worn hands and hopeful hearts as they seek the compassion of their spiritual master.

The Devotee of the Mystical Cup: Silent Pursuit of Divine Knowledge

In the eighth couplet, "مرید جام می" (devotee of the cup), Hafez identifies himself as a devotee of the mystical pursuit of divine love and knowledge. Though he gains profound insights, he remains silent about them, respecting their sacredness. He sends his message of devotion to the divine through the breeze, symbolizing the transmission of prayers and thoughts to the divine realm while maintaining the secrecy of his mystical experiences.

CHAPTER 23
GHAZAL 8: BE PATIENT

ساقیا برخیز و دَرِده جام را
خاک بر سر کن غم ایام را

ساغر می بر کفم نِه تا ز بَر
بَرکِشم این دلق اَزرَقفام را

گر چه بدنامیست نزد عاقلان
ما نمی‌خواهیم ننگ و نام را

باده دَرِده چند از این باد غرور

خاک بر سر نفس نافرجام را

دود آه سینهٔ نالان من
سوخت این افسردگان خام را

محرم راز دل شیدای خود
کس نمی‌بینم ز خاص و عام را

با دلارامی مرا خاطر خوش است
کز دلم یک باره بُرد آرام را

ننگرد دیگر به سرو اندر چمن
هرکه دید آن سرو سیم‌اندام را

صبر کن حافظ به سختی روز و شب
عاقبت روزی بیابی کام را

GHAZAL 8: BE PATIENT

Oh, cupbearer, rise and pour the wine, be patient,
  Dust your head with the sorrow of days, be patient.

Place the goblet of wine in my palm, so from this garment,
  I might strip away the disguise, the indigo fame, and be patient.

Though among the wise this may bring disrepute,
  We do not seek name or fame, for we are patient.

Pour wine – enough with this wind of pride!
  Cast dust upon this unfulfilled aim, and be patient.

The smoke of sighs that rise from my grieving heart,
  has burned the raw, the inexperienced — but be patient.

I am the confidante of the secrets of my enamored heart,
  I see no one, neither friend nor foe — thus I remain patient.

With that friend who brings be peace, my heart finds comfort,
  with the one ,who in a moment can steal my calm, I can be patient.

They will look no more at the cypresses in the grassy field,
  Whoever saw that tall slender figure, so be patient.

Endure, Hafez, through the hardships of night and day,
  Eventually, you shall attain your desire, so be patient.

COMMENTARY

Patience and Resilience in Hafez's Ghazal: Embracing Life's Transience

Hafez's ghazal beautifully explores the themes of patience, the transient nature of life, and the pursuit of inner peace and resilience. Each couplet introduces a new dimension of patience, illustrating its necessity and transformative power in navigating life's challenges.

Cupbearer: The Symbol of Release

In the first couplet, "ساقیا" (Cupbearer), Hafez calls upon the cupbearer to rise and pour the wine, urging to fill the cup to the brim. This act symbolizes casting away life's fleeting sorrows and embracing patience. The wine represents a means to momentarily escape despair and find solace.

Blue Shroud: Lifting the Weight of Sorrow

In the second couplet, "دلق اَزرَقفام" (blue shroud), Hafez speaks of the weight of the world resting heavy in his hands. He suggests that the spirit of the wine can lift this blue shroud from the heart, again emphasizing the need for patience to overcome despair.

Sullied Name: Steadfastness Amidst Judgment

In the third couplet, "بدنامی" (sullied name), Hafez acknowledges that in the circles of wise men, their names might be sullied over time.

He advises disregarding their scorn or praise and holding one's course steadily, underscoring the importance of patience.

Airs of Pride: The Resignation of Ambitions

In the fourth couplet, "باد غرور" (airs of pride), Hafez toasts to the resignation of pride over fruitless ventures and dreams. He suggests learning patience over the dust of these unfulfilled ambitions.

Smoke of Laments: Lessons from Hardship

In the fifth couplet, "دود آه" (smoke of laments), Hafez describes the smoke rising from a heart entwined with silent laments. This smoke teaches even the greenest souls through fire and ash to be patient, illustrating the transformative power of enduring hardship.

Secret of a Passionate Heart: Composure Amongst All

In the sixth couplet, "راز دل شیدای" (secret of a passionate heart), Hafez laments the lack of a soul to bear witness to his unconfined thoughts. He advises maintaining composure and patience, whether among nobles or peasants alike.

Blissful Love: Accepting the Pain of Love

In the seventh couplet, "خاطر خوش" (blissful love), Hafez speaks of blissful love that has stolen the calm from his mind. As solace departs with the beloved, he whispers softly to himself to be patient, accepting the pain of love with grace.

Silver Form: The Unattainable Ideal

In the eighth couplet, "سرو سیم‌اندام" (silver form), Hafez describes an enchanting silver form beyond the meadow's cypress, urging to gaze upon it and be patient despite its unattainability.

Self-Reminders: Holding Onto Hope

In the final couplet, "صبر کن حافظ" (be patient, Hafez), Hafez addresses himself, reminding that through the darkest hours of night, he should cling to the hope of dawn's light. His heart's wish nears, and he must continue to be patient.

Through these verses, Hafez not only intertwines patience with resilience and acceptance but also urges the reader to embrace patience as a necessary virtue in the face of life's inevitable challenges and transience.

CHAPTER 24
GHAZAL 9: THE TIME OF YOUTH

رونق عهد شباب است دگر بُستان را

میرسد مژدهٔ گل بلبل خوش الحان را

ای صبا گر به جوانان چمن باز رَسی

خدمت ما برسان سرو و گل و ریحان را

گر چنین جلوه کند مغبچهٔ باده فروش

خاکروب در میخانه کنم مژگان را

ای که بر مه کشی از عَنبر سارا چوگان

مضطرب حال مگردان، من سرگردان را

ترسم این قوم که بر دُردکشان می‌خندند
در سر کار خرابات کنند ایمان را

یار مردان خدا باش که در کشتی نوح
هست خاکی که به آبی نخرد طوفان را

برو از خانهٔ گردون به در و نان مطلب
کان سیه کاسه در آخر بِکُشد مهمان را

هر که را خوابگه آخر مشتی خاک است
گو چه حاجت که به افلاک کشی ایوان را

ماه کنعانی من! مسند مصر آنِ تو شد
وقت آن است که بدرود کنی زندان را

حافظا می خور و رندی کن و خوش باش ولی
دام تزویر مکن چون دگران قرآن را

GHAZAL 9: THE TIME OF YOUTH

The garden is shining with the energy of the time of youth right now
    The nightingale, with the sweetest melodies, brings news of the flowers just now

O morning breeze, if ever you return to the youth in the meadow,
    Tell the cypress, the flower, and basil that we are at their service, from now

If the Magi wine-seller's children display such effulgence,
    I would sweep the dust in the tavern with my eyelashes, from now

You, who can strike the moon with an amber polo-stick,
    Do not send me into such a frenzy; for I am already bewildered, right now

I fear that those people who ridicule the wine-drinkers, might be
    the ones who in the very end, ruin their own faith, from now

Be a friend of God's closest ones, for in Noah's Ark, there was a patch of earth, Noah himself who considered the entire flood as insignificant as a drop of water, you know

This revolving sky has a door. Go to it, but don't beg for bread,
For in the end, that begging bowl will undoubtedly poison the guest, you know

Tell those whose final resting place is but a handful of dust,
What use is it to try to extend your balcony to the heavens? you know

My beautiful moon! The throne of Egypt is yours,
It is time for you to bid farewell to prison, from now.

Hafez, drink wine and be happy, walk the path of the *Rend*, but
Do not – like others have, turn the Quran into a trap of deceit – *never and not now.*

GHAZAL 9: V2 THE TIME OF YOUTH

Here is a translation with a different radif equally emphasized:

The garden's age of youth blooms anew, avoid hypocrisy,
　The nightingale's joyous song brings news of roses, avoid hypocrisy.

O breeze, if you visit the young in the meadow,
　Serve us too, with cypress, rose, and basil, avoid hypocrisy.

If such charm the young wine-seller displays,
　I'd sweep the tavern's floor with my eyelashes, avoid hypocrisy.

You who draw the moon with a polo stick of amber,
　Do not disturb my perplexed state, avoid hypocrisy.

I fear those who mock the drinkers,
　Might in sacred ruins, forsake their faith, avoid hypocrisy.

Be among God's chosen in Noah's ark,
　For the earth there is not touched by the flood, avoid hypocrisy.

Leave the spinning celestial house asking not for bread,
    For the one in dark robes will betray the guest, avoid hypocrisy.

Everyone's final resting place is but a handful of dust,
    Why then pull the heavens to your porch? Avoid hypocrisy.

O my Canaanite moon! The throne of Egypt is now yours,
    It's time to bid the prison farewell, avoid hypocrisy.

Hafez, drink wine, live freely, be joyful, but
    Avoid laying traps of deceit like others, by the Qur'an, avoid hypocrisy.

COMMENTARY

Youth, Devotion, Humility, and Spiritual Wisdom in Hafez's Ghazal

Hafez's ghazal intricately weaves themes of youth, devotion, humility, and spiritual wisdom, guiding the reader through a profound exploration of life's transient beauty and the deeper truths of spiritual existence.

Vibrancy of Youth: Celebrating Spring's Renewal

In the first couplet, "عهد شباب" (time of youth), Hafez captures the essence of youth with the garden shining brightly, and he invites the nightingale to sing of the flowers' beauty, symbolizing the renewal and vibrancy of spring.

Devotion to Nature: The Connection Through the Morning Breeze

In the second couplet, "صبا" (morning breeze), Hafez's request to the morning breeze to convey his service to the natural elements if it returns to the youth in the meadow underscores his deep devotion and desire to remain connected to the beauty of nature.

Humility Before Beauty: Reverence for Radiance

In the third couplet, "مغبچهٔ باده فروش" (Magi wine-seller's children), Hafez expresses his deep admiration for the radiance of the wine-seller's children, showing his humility by saying he would sweep the tavern's floor with his eyelashes, an act of reverence for their luminous presence.

Overwhelmed by Beauty: The Striking Amber

In the fourth couplet, "عنبر سارا" (amber), Hafez communicates his bewilderment in the face of overwhelming beauty, as he addresses someone capable of striking the moon with a polo stick of amber, cautioning them about the disorienting effect of their charm.

Critique of Hypocrisy: Defending the Wine-Drinkers

In the fifth couplet, "خرابات" (wine-drinkers), Hafez voices his concern that those mocking the wine-drinkers might ultimately compromise their own faith, criticizing superficial judgments and hypocrisy.

Unwavering Faith: Advice from Noah's Ark

In the sixth couplet, "یار مردان خدا" (friend of God's men), Hafez advises aligning oneself with the steadfast and unwavering believers, akin to a steadfast patch of earth on Noah's Ark that withstands the storm, emphasizing the importance of strong faith.

Worldly Futility: The Revolving Sky's Deception

In the seventh couplet, "خانهٔ گردون" (revolving sky), Hafez warns against seeking worldly gains from the heavens, metaphorically described as a dark bowl that will ultimately betray the seeker, highlighting the futility of worldly pursuits.

Accepting Mortality: The Inevitability of Death

In the eighth couplet, "خوابگه آخر" (final resting place), Hafez reflects on the futility of material ambitions when everyone's ultimate end is just a handful of dust, questioning the need for excessive worldly striving.

Liberation and Greatness: The Canaanite Moon

In the ninth couplet, "ماه کنعانی" (Canaanite moon), Hafez celebrates a moment of liberation and greatness, telling his beloved that the throne of Egypt is now theirs, symbolizing a release from constraints and the attainment of a higher state.

Sincerity in Spiritual Journey: The Path of the Rend

In the final couplet, "رندی" (Rend), Hafez counsels joy and authenticity in one's spiritual journey, urging adherence to the path of the

Rend—a symbol of those who are spiritually intoxicated—and warns against using religion as a facade for deceit.

Through these verses, Hafez not only celebrates life's ephemeral beauties but also underscores the enduring values of humility, devotion, and the pursuit of genuine spiritual wisdom, all while cautioning against the pitfalls of hypocrisy and superficiality.

CHAPTER 25
GHAZAL 10: TOWARDS THE TAVERN

دوش از مسجد سوی میخانه آمد پیر ما

چیست یاران طریقت بعد از این تدبیر ما

ما مریدان روی سوی قبله چون آریم؟ چون

روی سوی خانهٔ خَمّار دارد پیر ما

در خرابات طریقت ما به هم منزل شویم

کاین چنین رفتهست در عهد ازل تقدیر ما

عقل اگر داند که دل در بند زلفش چون خوش است

عاقلان دیوانه گردند از پی زنجیر ما

روی خوبت آیتی از لطف بر ما کشف کرد
زان زمان جز لطف و خوبی نیست در تفسیر ما

با دل سنگینت آیا هیچ درگیرد شبی؟
آه آتشناک و سوز سینهٔ شبگیر ما

تیر آه ما ز گردون بگذرد حافظ خموش
رحم کن بر جان خود پرهیز کن از تیر ما

GHAZAL 10: TOWARDS THE TAVERN

Last night, our elder left the mosque, and towards the tavern he sped,
    In divine sanctums or in earthly realms, to which are we led?

How to the East do we bow, when his gaze is to the West?
    By the call to the prayer or by wine's song, to which are we led?

In the taverns of the spiritual path, we will dwell together,
    For such was decreed in the eternal covenant, from which we are led.

Reason knows little of a heart's rapture, ensnared and blind,
    By wisdom's light or love's trance, where are we led?

Your face, a verse of grace, has left a lasting trace in mind,
    In divine beauty or worldly charm, where are we led?

Hafiz, with sighs that reach the skies, in silence do confide,
    To heavens high or earth's embrace, where are we led?

COMMENTARY

Through these verses, Hafez weaves a complex tapestry of spiritual inquiry, challenging the reader to consider the true path of their spiritual and worldly pursuits, and the nature of the conflicts and tensions they navigate in their quest for understanding and truth.

Spiritual Conflict and the Quest for Divine Truth in Hafez's Ghazal

Hafez's ghazal offers a profound exploration of spiritual conflict, the search for divine truth, and the enduring tension between reason and love. Each couplet delves deeper into these themes, challenging conventional beliefs and inviting introspection on the true essence of one's spiritual journey.

Departure from Orthodoxy: The Path to the Tavern

In the first couplet, "پیر" (elder), Hafez describes an elder who abandons the mosque to lead the way to the tavern, symbolizing a shift from traditional religious practices to a pursuit of mystical spirituality. This raises questions about the destination of such a path—whether it leads to divine enlightenment or remains grounded in earthly experiences.

Contradiction in Devotion: East and West

In the second couplet, "قبله" (East) and "خمّار" (wine-seller), Hafez reflects on the inherent contradiction of facing East for prayer while being drawn westward towards the tavern. This juxtaposition highlights the conflict between adhering to traditional religious norms and embracing the allure of mysticism and earthly pleasures.

Predestined Fate: Ruins of Faith

In the third couplet, "خرابات" (ruins of faith), Hafez speaks of encountering a destined fate among the ruins of faith, suggesting a preordained intertwining of celestial and earthly fates. This metaphor questions the ultimate direction of their spiritual journey—whether it leads to ruin or redemption.

Limitations of Reason: The Heart's Rapture

In the fourth couplet, "عقل" (reason) and "دل" (heart), Hafez contemplates the inability of reason to grasp the heart's profound joy when captivated by love. He proposes that if reason could understand this rapture, even the wise would abandon their sanity in pursuit of such overwhelming love.

Divine vs. Worldly Beauty: The Beloved's Face

In the fifth couplet, "روی خویت" (your face), Hafez is captivated by the beloved's face, which he describes as a verse of grace that marks his soul. He ponders whether this enchantment stems from divine beauty or mere worldly allure, questioning the nature of his own admiration.

Unrequited Love: The Hard Heart

In the sixth couplet, "دل سنگینت" (your hard heart), Hafez expresses doubt whether his heartfelt sighs and the torment they bring will ever soften the beloved's unyielding heart. This couplet illustrates his deep longing and the emotional strife of unrequited love.

Sighs to the Heavens: Spiritual and Emotional Quest

In the final couplet, "آه" (sighs), Hafez depicts his sighs ascending to the skies, confiding in the silence of the cosmos. He wonders if his spiritual yearnings elevate him to heavenly realms or if he remains bound to the earthly domain, reflecting on the depth of his spiritual and emotional explorations.

CHAPTER 26
GHAZAL 11: I WILL LIGHT UP THE WORLD

ساقی به نور باده برافروز جامِ ما
مطرب بگو که کارِ جهان شُد به کامِ ما

ما در پیاله عکس رخ یار دیدهایم
ای بیخبر ز لذتِ شربِ مدامِ ما

هرگز نمیرد آن که دلش زنده شد به عشق
ثبت است بر جریدهٔ عالم دوامِ ما

چندان بُوَد کرشمه و نازِ سَهیقدان

کآید به جلوه سرو صنوبرخرام ما

ای باد اگر به گلشن اَحباب بگذری
زنهار عرضه ده بَر جانان پیام ما

اگو نام ما ز یاد به عمداً چه می‌بری؟!
خود آید آن که یاد نیاری ز نام ما

مستی به چشمِ شاهدِ دلبندِ ما خوش است
زآن رو سپرده‌اند به مستی زمام ما

ترسم که صرفه‌ای نَبَرَد روز بازخواست
نانِ حلالِ شیخ، ز آب حرام ما

حافظ ز دیده، دانهٔ اشکی همی‌فشان
باشد که مرغِ وصل کُند قصدِ دام ما

دریای اخضر فلک و کشتی هلال
هستند غرق نعمت حاجی‌قوام ما

GHAZAL 11: I WILL LIGHT UP THE WORLD

Saghi, go ahead, use the light of wine to illuminate our cup of love,
   Musician, sing the ballad, that the way of the world favors us now,
with a cup of love.

Know this: that in the goblet, we've seen the reflection of the beloved's
face:
   You, who are unaware of the bliss that resides in the cup of love.

They never die, those whose hearts have been enlivened by love
   We are inscribed forever upon the world's tablet, by the cup of love.

The coquettishness and charm of the tall beloved ones only last until
our cypress-like beloved reveals herself
   All others lose their allure, once she displays her beauty, by the cup
of love.

O wind, if you pass through the garden of Friends,
   Deliver my message to the beloved, with this cup of love.

Why would you intentionally erase my name from memory, when

there will come a time when no-one remembers me, but by cup of love.

That drunken-eye-look really looks good on our beloved,
   That's why I have taken the drunken path of the cup of love.

I fear that on the Day of Reckoning, the pious bread of the Sheikh will hold no merit compared to our forbidden wine with our cup of love.

Hafez, from your eyes, let fall a single tear, in hopes that,
   the bird of union may be drawn into our trap with this cup of love.

The green sea of the heavens and the crescent moon's ship are all drowned in the blessings of our benefactor,
   Haji Qavam — even the heavens and stars are overwhelmed by his generosity in that cup of love.

COMMENTARY

Hafez's ghazal masterfully explores the profound dimensions of love, spirituality, and the perpetual nature of true affection, utilizing vivid imagery and metaphorical language to convey the depth of these themes. Through these verses, the Rend poet weaves a complex narrative of love's transformative power, its spiritual dimensions, and its ability to endure beyond the mundane, urging the reader to embrace the mystical journey of love that resonates through all aspects of existence.

Illumination Through Love: The Cupbearer's Role

In the first couplet, "ساقی" (Saghi), Hafez invokes the cupbearer to fill the cup with wine, symbolizing enlightenment and joy brought about by love and spiritual ecstasy. This act sets the stage for a celebration of divine love, suggesting a moment when the world aligns favorably, illuminated by the "cup of love."

Divine Reflection: The Goblet of Love

In the second couplet, "پیاله" (goblet), Hafez sees the reflection of the beloved's face in the goblet, symbolizing the blissful and divine beauty within the cup of love. This profound encounter with the beloved's reflection emphasizes the deep, mystical experience of love, which remains unknown to those who have not felt its power.

Immortality of Love: Eternal Revival

In the third couplet, "عشق" (love), Hafez speaks of the immortality bestowed by love, suggesting that those revived by love live eternally. This spiritual immortality, recorded in the world's annals, highlights the timeless and enduring nature of true love.

Enduring Beauty: The Dance of the Cypress

In the fourth couplet, "سَهیقدان" (graceful ones), Hafez contrasts the fleeting beauty of the graceful with the perpetual dance of the cypress tree, stirred by the tune of the cup of love. This imagery underscores the enduring nature of love and beauty that outlasts physical appearances.

The Singular Message: The Wind's Task

In the fifth couplet, "باد" (wind), Hafez entrusts the wind with a message if it passes through the garden of friends—to carry only the essence of the cup of love. This emphasizes the centrality and over-whelming importance of love in his poetic message.

Indelible Memory: The Name in Love

In the sixth couplet, "نام" (name), Hafez reflects on the indelible impact of true love, asserting that despite efforts to erase his name, it will always be remembered in the context of the cup of love, symbol-izing the enduring memory of genuine affection.

Intoxicating Gaze: Drunken Delight

In the seventh couplet, "مستی" (drunkenness), Hafez revels in the sight of his beloved's drunken eyes, viewing this state as a blissful entrustment to the path of the cup of love. This couplet illustrates the joy and allure found in the beloved's intoxicating presence.

Spiritual Conflict: Day of Reckoning

In the eighth couplet, "روز بازخواست" (day of reckoning), Hafez expresses concern that conventional piety might not measure up against the mystical ecstasy of divine love during the final judgment, highlighting the tension between traditional religious practices and the unorthodox paths of mysticism.

Mystical Union: The Allure of Tears

In the ninth couplet, "اشک" (tear), Hafez suggests that shedding a tear in hope of union might draw the bird of union to the trap of the cup of love, symbolizing the powerful attraction and longing for a spiritual reunion with the beloved.

Cosmic Love: The Emerald Sky

In the final couplet, "دریای اخضر فلک" (emerald sky), Hafez expands the scope of love to the cosmos, describing how the emerald sky and the crescent moon are submerged in the grace of the cup of love. This grand imagery signifies the all-encompassing nature of divine love that transcends earthly and celestial boundaries.

CHAPTER 27
GHAZAL 12: LIGHT OF THE MOON

ای فروغِ ماهِ حُسن، از روی رخشان شما
آبروی خوبی از چاه زَنَخدان شما

عزم دیدار تو دارد جانِ بر لب آمده
باز گردد یا برآید؟ چیست فرمان شما؟

کَس به دور نرگست طرفی نبست از عافیت
بِه که نفروشند مستوری به مستان شما

بخت خواب آلود ما بیدار خواهد شد مگر

زان که زد بر دیده آبی، روی رخشان شما

با صبا همراه بفرست از رخِ گل دسته‌ای
بو که بویی بشنویم از خاکِ بستان شما

عمرتان باد و مراد ای ساقیانِ بزمِ جم
گر چه جام ما نشد پُر مِی به دوران شما

دل خرابی می‌کند، دلدار را آگه کنید
زینهار ای دوستان جان من و جان شما

کی دهد دست این غرض یا رب که همدستان شوند
خاطر مجموعِ ما، زلف پریشان شما

دور دار از خاک و خونِ دامن، چو بر ما بگذری
کاندر این ره کشته بسیارند، قربان شما

می‌کند حافظ دعایی، بشنو، آمینی بگو
روزی ما باد لعل شَکَّرافشان شما

ای صبا با ساکنانِ شهرِ یزد از ما بگو
کای سر حق ناشناسان گوی چوگان شما

گر چه دوریم از بساط قرب، همت دور نیست
بندهٔ شاه شماییم و ثناخوان شما

ای شَهنشاه بلند اختر، خدا را همتی

تا ببوسم همچو اختر خاک ایوان شما

GHAZAL 12: LIGHT OF THE MOON

O radiant moon of beauty, from **your** shining face,
  The honor of goodness draws from the dimple of **your** chin.

A soul on the on the verge of crossing over yearns to see you,
  So should it live or die? What is **your** command?

No one around your narcissus-like eyes has gained any benefit from playing it safe.
  It's better not to feign false piety to **your** intoxicated ones.

Perhaps our luck, so sleepy, will yet awaken, as you awaken us
  When water was splashed to wash our eyes, we saw **your** shining face.

Send with the breeze a bouquet from your flowers,
  Hoping to catch a scent from **your** garden's soil.

May your life and wishes be blessed, O cupbearers of Jam's feast,
  though our cup remained empty of wine in **your** era.

My heart is in distress; let the beloved know,

for mercy's sake friends, for my soul and **yours**.

O Lord, will this desire ever be fulfilled, that they unite,
  Our composed thoughts coherent, and **your** disheveled hair?

Lift your hem from dust and blood as you pass by,
  For many have perished on this path, sacrificed in **your** devotion.

When Hafez prays, listen deeply and say amen,
  May the sugar-scattering ruby of **yours** be our fate.

O morning breeze, go tell the residents of Yazd on our behalf,
  That the heads of the ungrateful; their heads are **your** polo ball.

Though we are far from your court, our efforts do not make us distant,
  We are the servants of our king and the singers of **your** praise.

O King of kings, I pray God grants me the power
  So, I may kiss the dust of **your** porch as do the stars.

COMMENTARY

Through this ghazal, Hafez intricately captures the essence of human emotions bound by love and longing, weaving a tapestry of poetic expressions that resonate with the universal quest for divine beauty and understanding.

Exploring Love, Longing, and Divine Beauty in Hafez's Hafez's ghazal beautifully navigates through the intertwined themes of love, intense longing, and the pursuit of divine beauty, each couplet unfolding deep emotional landscapes through rich metaphors and evocative imagery.

Celestial Beauty: The Radiance of the Moon

In the first couplet, "فروغِ ماهِ حُسن" (radiant moon), Hafez compares the beloved's brilliant face to the radiant moon, suggesting that the beloved's beauty enhances the moon's natural splendor. This metaphor not only elevates the beloved's beauty to celestial levels but also highlights the transformative effect of their presence on the surrounding world.

Desperate Yearning: Life on the Edge

In the second couplet, "جانِ بر لب آمده" (soul at the brink), Hafez portrays his soul as teetering on the brink of existence, desperate for a glimpse of the beloved. This image conveys the profound longing and the life-or-death intensity of his love, where seeing the beloved is essential for his survival.

Irresistible Allure: The Danger of Enchantment

In the third couplet, "عافیت" (well-being) and "مستان" (intoxicated ones), Hafez reflects on the overwhelming allure of the beloved's charm, which no one can escape. He warns against selling one's dignity to those intoxicated by love, acknowledging the destructive potential of such overwhelming beauty.

Hope and Revival: Awakening Fortune

In the fourth couplet, "بخت خواب آلود" (luck shrouded in slumber), Hafez holds onto a sliver of hope that his dormant luck might awaken with the radiance of the beloved's face, akin to water reviving a sleeper. This couplet symbolizes his hope for rejuvenation and good fortune through the beloved's transformative beauty.

Symbolic Gestures: The Scent of Solace

In the fifth couplet, "صبا" (morning breeze) and "گل دستهای" (bouquet), Hafez requests the morning breeze to bring a bouquet from the beloved's garden, longing for any trace of the beloved that might offer comfort and joy.

Generosity Amidst Despair: Unfulfilled Yet Kind

In the sixth couplet, "عمرتان باد" (may your life be blessed), Hafez extends a blessing to the lives of cupbearers, displaying his selflessness and generosity despite his own unfulfilled desires.

Emotional Turmoil: Seeking Compassion

In the seventh couplet, "دل خرابی" (heart in ruins), Hafez implores his friends to convey the dire state of his heart to the beloved, emphasizing the critical need for the beloved's awareness and compassion towards his emotional distress.

Collective Longing: Unity in Desire

In the eighth couplet, "همدستان" (companions) and "زلف پریشان" (disheveled locks), Hafez yearns for the fulfillment of his desires with the aid of companions, illustrating how the beloved's captivating beauty unites them in shared longing.

Perilous Path: Sacrificial Devotion

In the ninth couplet, "دامن" (hem) and "خون" (blood), Hafez warns the beloved to keep their hem away from the ground stained with the blood of those who have sacrificed for love, indicating the perilous journey of love. This emphasizes the dangerous and sacrificial nature of the path, marked by the numerous lives lost in devotion to the beloved.

Divine Prayer: Seeking Blessings

In the tenth couplet, "دعایی" (prayer) and "آمین" (Amen), Hafez offers a heartfelt prayer, asking for the beloved's sweet and ruby-like lips to be his fate. He emphasizes the importance of this prayer being heard and affirmed.

Message to the Beloved: Conveying Longing

In the eleventh couplet, "صبا" (morning breeze) and "یزد" (Yazd), Hafez asks the morning breeze to convey his message to the inhabitants of Yazd, highlighting the beloved's dominion over those who do not appreciate their blessings.

Unwavering Devotion: Servants and Singers

In the twelfth couplet, "بنده" (servant) and "ثناخوان" (praise singers), Hafez reaffirms his unwavering devotion to the beloved, declaring that despite physical distance, their efforts and praises remain close and sincere.

Divine Aspiration: Kissing the Porch

In the final couplet, "خدا را همتی" (for God's sake, grant the power) and "ایوان" (porch), Hafez prays for the strength to kiss the dust of the beloved's porch, comparing this humble act to the stars kissing the earth, signifying his deep respect and longing for the divine presence.

CHAPTER 28
GHAZAL 13: DEWDROPS GRACE THE TULIP'S FACE

می‌دمد صبح و کلّه بست سحاب
الصَّبوح الصَّبوح یا اصحاب

می‌چکد ژاله بر رخِ لاله
المُدام المُدام یا احباب

می‌وزد از چمن نسیمِ بهشت
هان، بنوشید دَم به دَم می‌ی ناب

تخت زُمُرّد زده است گل به چمن

راحِ چون لعلِ آتشین دریاب

درِ میخانه بسته‌اند دگر
اِفتَتِح یا مُفَتِّح الاَبواب

لب و دَندانْت را حقوق نمک
هست بر جان و سینه‌هایِ کباب

این چنین موسمی عجب باشد
که ببندند میکده به شتاب

بر رخِ ساقیِ پری پیکر
همچو حافظ بنوش بادهٔ ناب

GHAZAL 13: DEWDROPS GRACE THE TULIP'S FACE

Dawn breathes through the tightly bound veil of clouds as we rise
    Dear Friends, "Morning's here! Morning's here!" it's time to rise

Glistening dewdrops grace the tulip's radiant face,
    Dearly beloved, "Pour the wine! Pour the wine!" it's time to rise

A breeze of paradise reaches us from the grassy meadow,
    Listen! Savor the wine sip by sip, for it's time to rise.

The flowers have set emerald thrones in grassy fields,
    Seek that ruby-like wine, with fire inside, for it's time to rise.

Alas, the tavern is closed and its doors have been shut
    O Opener of doors! Please help us open its doors, for its time to rise.

Salt's rights that came from your teeth and lips
    Are etched on the body and soul of the kebab! It's time to rise!

In such a season it would seem strange indeed,

That they would shut the tavern so early. It's time to rise!

While witnessing the face of the angelic cupbearer,
    Learn to drink the pristine wine, like Hafez, for it's time to rise.

COMMENTARY

This ghazal by Hafez is a rich tapestry of imagery and emotion, celebrating the ephemeral beauty of life through nature, wine, and companionship. It is a call to appreciate the fleeting moments, to rise and truly live amidst the wonders of each new dawn.

Awakening to New Possibilities: The Break of Dawn

In the first couplet, "می‌دمد صبح و کلّه بست سحاب" (Dawn breathes through the tightly bound veil of clouds), Hafez captures the moment of dawn breaking through the clouds, symbolizing a fresh start and the awakening of new possibilities. He calls his friends to rise, imbuing the scene with a sense of urgency and excitement to embrace the new day.

Nature's Elegance: Dew and Tulips

In the second couplet, "می‌چکد ژاله بر رخِ لاله" (Glistening dewdrops grace the tulip's radiant face), Hafez paints a vivid picture of morning dew on tulips, symbolizing purity and the fresh beauty of nature. He ties this image to the act of pouring wine, suggesting a celebration that mirrors the natural beauty around them.

Divine Breezes: The Meadow's Gift

In the third couplet, "می‌وزد از چمن نسیم بهشت" (A breeze of paradise reaches us from the grassy meadow), the poet describes a heavenly breeze that stirs the senses, enhancing the enjoyment of wine. This coupling of nature's breath with the sipping of wine deepens the connection to a paradisiacal state.

Regal Nature: Emerald Thrones in the Meadow

In the fourth couplet, "تخت زُمُرُد زده است گل به چمن" (The flowers have set emerald thrones in grassy fields), Hafez speaks to the grandeur of nature, where flowers create majestic scenes akin to emerald thrones. This regal imagery is juxtaposed with the pursuit of passionate, fiery wine, enhancing the celebratory tone.

Momentary Setback: The Closed Tavern

In the fifth couplet, "درِ میخانه بستهاند دگر" (the tavern is closed and its doors have been shut), a twist occurs with the closure of the tavern, a central place of joy and communion. Hafez calls upon the "Opener of doors" to restore access, symbolizing a plea for the return of joyful gatherings.

Sensual Pleasures: Salt from Lips and Teeth

In the sixth couplet, "لب و دَندانْت را حقوق نمک" (Salt's rights that came from your teeth and lips), the poet playfully references the saltiness from the beloved's lips, likening it to the flavor enhancing a meal. This metaphor highlights the intimate and sensual pleasures of love, akin to the enjoyment of food and wine.

Celebratory Surprise: Questioning the Early Closure

In the seventh couplet, "این چنین موسمی عجب باشد" (In such a season it would seem strange indeed), Hafez expresses disbelief and humor over the tavern's early closure during such a festive season, emphasizing the natural human desire to celebrate life's abundant moments.

Learning from the Cupbearer: Embracing the Moment

In the final couplet, "بر رخِ ساقی پری پیکر" (While witnessing the face of the angelic cupbearer), Hafez concludes by urging his audience to emulate his approach to enjoying wine and life, particularly in the presence of the angelic cupbearer, a figure embodying divine grace and beauty.

CHAPTER 29
GHAZAL 14: THE STATE OF WONDER

گفتم ای سلطانِ خوبان رحم کن بر این غریب
گفت در دنبالِ دل، رَه گم کُنَد مسکین غریب

گفتمش مَگذر زمانی، گفت معذورم بدار
خانه پروردی، چه تاب آرد غم چندین غریب

خفته بر سنجابِ شاهی نازنینی را چه غم؟
گر ز خار و خاره سازد بستر و بالین غریب

ای که در زنجیرِ زلفت جایِ چندین آشناست

خوش فتاد آن خالِ مشکین بر رخِ رنگین غریب

مینماید عکسِ می، در رنگِ رویِ مَه وَشَت
همچو برگِ ارغوان بر صفحهٔ نسرین، غریب

بس غریب افتاده است آن مور خَط، گردِ رُخَت
گر چه نَبوَد در نگارستان، خطِ مشکین غریب

گفتم ای شامِ غریبان طُرّهٔ شبرنگِ تو
در سحرگاهان حذر کن، چون بنالد این غریب

گفت حافظ آشنایان در مقامِ حیرتند
دور نَبوَد گر نشیند خسته و مسکین غریب

GHAZAL 14: THE STATE OF WONDER

I said, "O Gracious King of Good, have mercy on this estranged one,
    He replied, "On the path of the heart, some may lose their way,
these poor estranged ones."

I told him, "Don't pass me by; wait a moment," he said, " Leave me be,
    For I, secluded by choice, cannot bear the burden of all these many
estranged ones."

What sorrow can the beloved feel, who sleeps on royal fur
    while they make their bed and pillow out of thorns and stones, the
estranged ones?

In the chains of your locks of hair, there is space for many familiar ones
    How well that dark mole rests on your colorful cheek, like an
estranged one

The reflection of wine appears on your moon-like face,
    Like a red leaf on a white page, an estranged one.

The ant-like line around your face appears so strange,

Though in the garden of images, a dark line is not an estranged one.

I said, O night of strangers, beware your dark tresses,
At dawn, take care, for they will wail, the estranged ones.

Many a lonely moth has fallen around your face, with a letter for your cheek,
Although it won't reach the narcissus garden, the ink of musk of the lovely estranged one.

I said, "O evening of strangers in separation, with your night-colored tresses,
Be cautious in the early morning, how this estranged one in laments separation.

Hafez said, "The Familiar ones are in a state of wonderment,
May it never happen that they sit as weary and poor, estranged ones.

———

I said, "O Sultan of beauties, have mercy on this stranger."
Said, "In pursuit of the heart, he might lose his way, the poor stranger ."

I said, "Don't pass me by," he said, "Excuse me."
"One raised in comfort cannot bear the sorrow of so many strangers."

What sorrow has the beloved, sleeping on the royal fur if the stranger makes his bed and pillow of thorns and stones.
O you, in whose chain of curls entangle the souls of the many familiars,
Your black mole looks beautiful to the colorful face of the stranger.

The reflection of wine appears in the color of your moon-like face, Like a crimson leaf on a page of white jasmine, like a stranger.

That ant-like down has fallen so strangely around your face, Although there is no black down in the garden of paintings, a stranger.

I said, "O night of strangers, your dark tresses, Beware in the early dawn, when this stranger cries out."

Hafez said, "The familiars are in a state of wonder. It is not far off that the weary and poor stranger may sit down."

Key Terms to Note:
- **Sultan of beauties:** A common way to address a beloved in Persian poetry.
- **Stranger (Gharib):** A central theme in the poem, referring to someone who is/feels out of place, and is longing for connection for the "familiar" for the "Friend."
- **Heart:** Symbolizes love and desire.
- **House-raised:** Someone who has lived a sheltered life.
- **Royal fur (Sanjab-e Shahi):** A symbol of luxury and comfort.
- **Black mole:** A traditional symbol of beauty.
- **Crimson leaf on white jasmine:** A metaphor for the beloved's blush.
- **Ant-like down:** Refers to the fine hair on the beloved's face.
- **Garden of paintings:** Refers to the idealized world of art.
- **Dark tresses:** A symbol of the night and the beloved's hair.
- **Hafez:** The takhalos, or mention of the poet himself, used at the ending stanza to introduce a wise observation.

COMMENTARY

Through this ghazal, Hafez not only captures the essence of estrangement but also celebrates the unique beauty and depth of the estranged soul. His use of rich metaphors and reflective insights calls for empathy and a deeper understanding of those who navigate the margins of society and love, highlighting the intrinsic value of their experiences.

The Estranged Seeker: A Plea for Compassion

In the first couplet, "غریب" (estranged one), Hafez addresses a gracious ruler, seeking mercy for those estranged. The ruler's response —that following one's heart might lead to being lost—underscores the vulnerability and risks faced by those who pursue love and connection, often finding themselves adrift.

Isolation Amidst Unsupportive Surroundings

In the second couplet, Hafez appeals to the ruler not to overlook him, even momentarily. The ruler's admission of his inability to provide relief to many estranged souls reflects the deep isolation experienced by those in environments ill-equipped to nurture their spiritual and emotional needs.

Loneliness at the Pinnacle

The third couplet reveals a beloved of high status confined to a bed of thorns and thistles, illustrating that elevation does not shield one from loneliness or estrangement. This suggests that external comforts do not necessarily translate into inner peace, highlighting the universal susceptibility to isolation.

Chains of Beauty: The Estranged Mole

In the fourth couplet, "زنجیر زلف" (locks like chains), the beloved's hair is described as chains, a metaphor for entrapment that links to many yet isolates the bearer. A charming mole, symbolizing an estranged beauty, emphasizes uniqueness and separation from the norm, adding depth to the theme of isolation.

Vivid Isolation: Wine and the Moon-like Face

The fifth couplet uses wine reflecting in the beloved's moon-like face to depict the estranged one's vivid yet isolated beauty. This metaphor of a crimson petal on a narcissus page enhances the notion of estrangement as both separate and essential to the overall allure.

The Lonely Moth: Unfulfilled Longing

In the sixth couplet, "تنها" (lonely), a moth drawn to the beloved's face symbolizes the lonely journey of the estranged, carrying a letter of devotion but unlikely to reach its destination. This poignant image of solitary devotion underlines the moth's—and by extension, the estranged's—unfulfilled longing.

The Pain of Separation: Night into Day

The seventh couplet portrays the evening of estrangement through night-colored tresses, warning of the morning's lament. This transition from night to day encapsulates the emotional trajectory of pain to hope, emphasizing the deep longing for reconnection.

Universal Estrangement: The Weary Familiar

In the final couplet, Hafez reflects on the familiar ones awed by their state of weariness and poverty, akin to that of the estranged. This revelation of a shared experience underscores the universality of estrangement, suggesting that isolation and exhaustion are common to all, regardless of their apparent belonging.

COMMENTARY ON TERMINOLOGY

In Sufism, the concept of "مقام" (maqam) refers to a spiritual station or level of consciousness that a seeker or Sufi aspirant progresses through on their journey toward God or spiritual enlightenment. These maqamat represent different stages of spiritual growth, understanding, and closeness to the Divine. Each maqam signifies a unique state of being, a deeper level of understanding, and an increased capacity for spiritual insight.

In the line "گفت حافظ آشنایان در مقام حیرتند" (Hafez said, 'Familiar ones are in a state of wonderment'), Hafez may be alluding to the idea that those who are spiritually advanced or familiar with higher maqamat are in a perpetual state of awe and wonderment in the face of the Divine. This can be seen as an acknowledgment of the ongoing spiritual journey and the recognition that the path to God is filled with continuous amazement, profound insights, and a sense of marvel at the mysteries of existence.

So, in the context of Sufism, this line can be interpreted as an affirmation of the spiritual journey and the profound experiences that those who traverse the maqamat encounter on their path toward spiritual realization and closeness to the Divine.

In the context of Sufism, "آشنایان" (ashnaayan) refers to the spiritually initiated, experienced, or those who have reached a certain level of understanding and insight within the Sufi tradition. These individuals are often referred to as "Sufis" or "mystics."

Here are some key points to elaborate on the term "آشنایان" (ashnaayan)in Sufism. For example, آشنایان (ashnaayan) represents individuals who have embarked on a profound spiritual journey, seeking to attain closeness to God and to experience the Divine in their lives. They are characterized by their dedication to inner transformation, their deep spiritual insights, and their commitment to living a life aligned with love, compassion, and Divine awareness.

- Spiritual Knowledge and Experience: Sufism places a strong emphasis on experiential knowledge of the Divine. Those who are considered آشنایان are individuals who have gained a deeper understanding of spiritual truths through direct personal experiences, often involving states of heightened consciousness, ecstasy, and mystical union with God.

- Inner Journey: Sufism is known for its focus on the inner journey of the soul toward God. آشنایان are individuals who have embarked on this inner journey with sincerity and dedication. They seek to purify their hearts, transcend worldly attachments, and draw closer to God through acts of devotion, prayer, meditation, and self-reflection.

- Mentorship and Guidance: Many آشنایان benefit from the guidance and mentorship of more advanced Sufi teachers or spiritual guides known as "shaykhs" or "pirs." These guides provide spiritual direction, share their experiences, and help their disciples navigate the challenges and stages of the spiritual path.

- States and Stages: In Sufism, there is a recognition of various spiritual states (ahwal) and stages (maqamat) that individuals may go through on their journey toward God. آشنایان are often associated with having reached specific states or stages characterized by a profound sense of spiritual awareness, humility, and love for God.

- Community and Brotherhood: Sufism often emphasizes the importance of community and spiritual brotherhood. آشنایان are part of a larger Sufi community where they can share their experiences, offer support and guidance to others, and collectively engage in practices that deepen their spiritual connection.

- Service and Love: آشنایان are often known for their selflessness, compassion, and love for all of creation. Their spiritual experiences lead them to serve others and to see the Divine presence in everything and everyone.

CHAPTER 30
GHAZAL 15: THE ARROW SHOT BY YOUR GLANCE

ای شاهد قدسی، که کَشَد بند نقابت؟
وی مرغ بهشتی، که دهَد دانه و آبت؟

خوابم بشد از دیده در این فکر جگرسوز
کآغوش که شد، منزل آسایش و خوابت؟

درویش نمی‌پرسی و ترسم که نباشد
اندیشۀ آمرزش و پروای ثوابت

راه دل عشاق زد آن چشم خماری

پیداست از این شیوه که مست است شرابت

تیری که زدی بر دلم از غمزه، خطا رفت
تا باز چه اندیشه کند رای صوابت

هر ناله و فریاد که کردم نشنیدی
پیداست نگارا که بلند است جَنابت

دور است سر آب از این بادیه، هش دار
تا غول بیابان نفریبد به سرابت

تا در ره پیری به چه آیین رَوی ای دل
باری به غلط صرف شد ایام شبابت

ای قصر دل افروز که منزلگه انسی
یا رب مَکُناد آفت ایام خرابت

حافظ نه غلامیست که از خواجه گریزد
صلحی کن و بازآ که خرابم ز عِتابت

CHAPTER 31
GHAZAL 15: THE ARROW SHOT BY YOUR GLANCE

O CELESTIAL BEAUTY, who will lift the veil from your face?
  O heavenly bird, who will provide you grain and water?
  Won't you come back?

Sleep has fled from my eyes in this heart-burning thought:
  Whose embrace has become the resting place of your comfort and sleep?
  Won't you come back?

You do not inquire about the dervish, and I fear
  That you do not think of forgiveness and care for your reward.
  Won't you come back?

That languid eye has taken the hearts of lovers;
  It is clear from this manner that your wine is intoxicating.
  Won't you come back?

· · ·

The arrow shot by your glance just missed my heart;
Won't you come back?
Let's see what your next thought or intention will be.
Won't you come back?

You did not hear any of my cries and laments;
It is clear, O beloved, that your rank is high.
Won't you come back?

The water source is far from this desert, beware;
Lest the desert demon deceive you with a mirage.
Won't you come back?

As you tread the path of old age, by what creed will you go, O heart?
Alas, your youthful days were spent in vain.
Won't you come back?

O heart-illuminating palace that is the dwelling of intimacy,
May the ruin of time never befall you, by God.
Won't you come back?

Hafez is not a disciple to flee from his master;
Make peace and return, for I am ruined by your rebuke.
Won't you come back?

COMMENTARY

Through this ghazal, Hafez tries to encapsulate the beauty, pain, and spiritual longing of love, using the beloved as a metaphor for divine beauty and the pursuit of spiritual truth. The poem richly illustrates the complex interplay between earthly desires and heavenly aspirations, capturing the soul's eternal quest for union and understanding.

Celestial Mystique: The Unveiled Divine

In the first couplet, "ای شاهد قدسی، که کَشَد بند نقابت؟" (O celestial beauty, who can release the bond of your veil?), Hafez portrays the beloved as a transcendent figure, whose hidden essence is like a bird of paradise—mysterious and nourished by divine sustenance. This sets a tone of awe and otherworldly allure, emphasizing the inscrutable nature of the beloved.

Sleepless Longing: Turmoil of the Heart

In the second couplet, "خوابم بشد از دیده در این فکر جگرسوز" (Sleep fled from my eyes in this heart-burning thought), the poet shares his sleepless nights, tormented by thoughts of who comforts the beloved. This vividly captures the pain of longing and the emotional distress of love that is felt rather than seen.

Spiritual Neglect: The Unanswered Dervish

In the third couplet, "درویش نمی‌پرسی و ترسم که نباشد" (You don't ask the dervish, and I fear, you have no concern), Hafez laments the beloved's disregard for the spiritual seeker. This neglect underscores a broader theme of spiritual estrangement and the fear that the beloved is indifferent to the lover's deeper spiritual needs.

Guidance Through Beauty: The Intoxicating Path

The fourth couplet, "راه دل عشاق زد آن چشم خماری" (The path of lovers' hearts is set by your intoxicating eyes), suggests that the beloved's captivating gaze dictates the course of the lovers' journeys. This metaphor of intoxication speaks to the overwhelming influence of the beloved's beauty, which mesmerizes and leads the heart astray.

Mistaken Glances: The Missed Mark

In the fifth couplet, "تیری که زدی بر دلم از غمزه، خطا رفت" (The arrow shot by your glance missed its mark), Hafez portrays the beloved's glance as an arrow—potent yet errant. This line explores the idea that even in her imperfection, there is a beauty and a cause for reflection, adding depth to the beloved's allure.

Unheard Cries: The Silent Suffering

In the sixth couplet, "هر ناله و فریاد که کردم نشنیدی" (Every cry and shout I made, you did not hear), the poet expresses frustration over his unheard lamentations, highlighting the beloved's distant and perhaps elevated status, which isolates her from the lover's suffering.

Cautionary Wisdom: Mirage of Love

The seventh couplet, "دور است سر آب از این بادیه، هش دار" (The source of water is far from this desert, beware), serves as a metaphorical warning about the illusions of fulfillment in love, likening the lover's quest to a perilous journey through a deceptive desert.

Regretful Reflections: The Wasted Youth

In the eighth couplet, "تا در ره پیری به چه آیین رَوی ای دل" (How shall you tread the path of old age, O heart?), Hafez contemplates the passage of time and the youth spent in vain pursuits, mourning the transient nature of early passions and the unreturned investments of the heart.

Transience of Joy: The Imperiled Abode

In the ninth couplet, "ای قصرِ دل افروز که منزلگه انسی" (O illuminating palace, the abode of human connection), the poet prays for the preservation of the beloved's dwelling, symbolizing the fragile joys and connections that are threatened by the ravages of time.

Loyal Devotion: The Unyielding Bond

The final couplet, "حافظ نه غلامیست که از خواجه گریزد" (Hafez is not a slave who would flee from his master), culminates in a declaration of steadfast loyalty. Hafez affirms his unwavering commitment to the beloved, regardless of the hardships or the reproach he faces.

CHAPTER 32
GHAZAL 16: TO CAST AWAY

WE PROVIDE two translations for this ghazal.

خَمی که ابروی شوخِ تو در کمان انداخت
به قصد جانِ منِ زارِ ناتوان انداخت

نبود نقش دو عالم، که رنگ الفت بود
زمانه طرح محبت، نه این زمان انداخت

به یک کرشمه که نرگس به خودفروشی کرد
فریبِ چشمِ تو صد فتنه در جهان انداخت

. . .

شراب خورده و خوی کرده میروی به چمن
که آبِ روی تو، آتش در ارغوان انداخت

به بزمگاهِ چمن دوش مست بگذشتم
چو از دهانِ توام غنچه در گمان انداخت

بنفشه طُرّهٔ مفتول خود گره میزد
صبا حکایتِ زلفِ تو در میان انداخت

ز شرمِ آن که به روی تو نسبتش کردم
سمن به دستِ صبا، خاک در دهان انداخت

من از ورع، مِی و مطرب ندیدمی زین پیش
هوای مغبچگانم در این و آن انداخت

کنون به آبِ مِی لعل، خرقه میشویم
نصیبهٔ ازل از خود، نمیتوان انداخت

مگر گشایش حافظ در این خرابی بود؟
که بخششِ ازلش، در می مغان انداخت

جهان به کامِ من اکنون شود، که دور زمان
مرا به بندگیِ خواجهٔ جهان انداخت

CHAPTER 33
GHAZAL 16: TO CAST AWAY

THE CURVE of your playful eyebrow pulled like a bow, and cast away,
   Something aimed right at my poor soul, to make it sway, to cast away.

The colors of affection was not part of the original design of the two worlds
   And these times have not designed it that away, but cast it away.

To its shame, the narcissus, with just a glance, was willing to give itself up.
   Your mischievous eyes have created a hundred conspiracies ready to cast away.

Intoxicated, to the meadow you go — a path you know well,
   the grace of your face, brought flames to the heart of the tulips, then cast them away.

.   .   .

Last night, through the garden's feast, inebriated, I made my way,
   buds of doubt, sprung within me, but your lips — they cast them
away.

As the violet, in silent homage was tying its curls, the breeze came
   And told it tales of your tresses' charm, and how it would cast them
away.

Comparing them to your grace, in shame, my complaints crumbled,
and
   the jasmine, aided by the hand of the wind, that dust, in humility, it
cast away.

Through piety, I did not dwell in wine and music before this
   Yet, desires for the tavern's beauties, took me there and piety, it cast
away.

Now, I wash my cloak with that ruby wine; for
   the destiny from eternity, one cannot cast away

Was it in this ruin that Hafez found his breakthrough?
   By Eternal Grace, a wine drinkers' fate, he was cast away.

At last, the world seems to be turning to my prosperity now that
   the cycle of time compels me to be a devotee of the master of
destiny.

COMMENTARY

Hafez's ghazal intricately weaves the themes of love, beauty, and destiny, showing how each element casts its influence on the soul, shaping experiences and perceptions. The repeated motif of being cast away underscores the transient nature of these experiences and the ever-changing dynamics of life and love.

Your Playful Eyebrow (ابروی شوخِ تو)

Hafez's ghazal reflects on themes of love, fate, and the interplay of beauty and desire. In the first couplet, Hafez compares the curve of the beloved's playful eyebrow to a bow. He states that it casts an arrow aimed at his weak soul, illustrating how the beloved's subtle gestures can deeply affect and destabilize him.

Color of Affection (رنگ الفت)

In the second couplet, Hafez observes that the original design of the two worlds did not include the color of affection. He reflects on how time has also cast away the essence of love, indicating that love is an elusive, timeless concept not rooted in the material world.

Glance (کرشمه)

In the third couplet, Hafez describes how a single mischievous glance from the beloved's eyes creates countless conspiracies, ready to cast away. This highlights the power and influence of the beloved's gaze, which can incite widespread turmoil and fascination.

Grace of Your Face (آبِ روی تو)

In the fourth couplet, Hafez describes the beloved proceeding to the meadow intoxicated, causing the tulips to be inflamed by the grace of the beloved's face, which is then cast away. This suggests that the beloved's presence ignites passion but also leaves behind a sense of desolation.

Bud of Doubt (غنچه در گمان)

In the fifth couplet, Hafez recounts his inebriated journey through the garden's feast, where a doubt blossomed within him, cast away by the beloved's lips. This reflects the confusion and uncertainty that love can create, even in moments of joy.

Curls of the Violet (طرِّه مفتول)

In this sixth couplet, Hafez notes how the violet ties its curls in homage, while the breeze spreads tales of the beloved's tresses' charm, casting them amongst the people. This symbolizes the far-reaching influence of the beloved's beauty, which is admired and revered by nature itself.

Jasmine (سمن)

In the seventh couplet, Hafez mentions that in shame, his comparisons to the beloved made the jasmine cast its dust to the wind. This portrays how even the most beautiful elements of nature feel humbled and inadequate compared to the beloved.

Piety (ورع)

In the eighth couplet, Hafez reflects on his past piety, noting how unseen desires for beauty cast him from one place to another. This suggests an internal struggle between spiritual aspirations and earthly desires.

Cloak (خرقه)

In the ninth couplet, Hafez talks about cleansing his cloak with wine's ruby water in hope to quell his eternal fate, which cannot be cast away. This indicates his attempt to reconcile with his destiny through the symbolic act of purification with wine.

Opening or Breakthrough for Hafez (کشایش حافظ)

In the tenth couplet, Hafez wonders if his salvation lies in the ruin, as eternal grace has cast him into the fate of the wine drinkers. This reflects the idea that true enlightenment and freedom may come from embracing life's imperfections and vices.

Devotee of the Lord of destiny / World's Lord (بندگیِ خواجهٔ جهان)

In the final couplet, Hafez acknowledges that the world now seems to favor him as the cycle of time has cast him into servitude of the world's lord. This signifies his acceptance of his role and destiny, finding contentment in his place in the world.

CHAPTER 34
GHAZAL 16: TO CAST AWAY (2ND)

HERE IS THE SECOND TRANSLATION.

خَمی که ابروی شوخِ تو در کمان انداخت
به قصد جانِ منِ زارِ ناتوان انداخت

نبود نقش دو عالم، که رنگ الفت بود
زمانه طرح محبت، نه این زمان انداخت

به یک کرشمه که نرگس به خودفروشی کرد
فریبِ چشمِ تو صد فتنه در جهان انداخت

شراب خورده و خوی کرده میروی به چمن
که آبِ روی تو، آتش در ارغوان انداخت

به بزمگاهِ چمن دوش مست بگذشتم
چو از دهانِ توام غنچه در گمان انداخت

. . .

بنفشه طُرّه مفتول خود گره می‌زد

صبا حکایتِ زلفِ تو در میان انداخت

ز شرمِ آن که به روی تو نسبتش کردم

سمن به دستِ صبا، خاک در دهان انداخت

من از ورع، مِی و مطرب ندیدمی زین پیش

هوای مغبچگانم در این و آن انداخت

کنون به آبِ مِی لعل، خرقه می‌شویم

نصیبهٔ ازل از خود، نمی‌توان انداخت

مگر گشایش حافظ در این خرابی بود؟

که بخششِ ازلش، در می مغان انداخت

جهان به کامِ من اکنون شود، که دورِ زمان

مرا به بندگیِ خواجهٔ جهان انداخت

GHAZAL 16: TO CAST AWAY (2ND)

The curve that your playful eyebrow into its bow, has cast
    Was intended to shoot me, the poor, the helpless soul, at last

It was not in the design of either world, to be the color of affection
    But Love was designed in this era, and into eternity was cast

With a glance that made the narcissus parade itself for sale
    The mischief of your eyes has a hundred seditions to cast

Having drunk wine and adopted its ways, you go to the meadow
    For your modesty has into the tulip, a fire cast

I passed drunk through the meadow's gathering place last night
    As from your mouth, that I like a bud, into doubt, was cast

The violet was so busy tying its twisted locks
    When the morning breeze, into your locks, did tales cast

From its shame, when I attributed it to your face, the jasmine
    By the hand of the morning breeze, dust in its mouth did cast

Out of piety, I had not seen wine nor musicians before this
    The desire to venture around, the young tavern-goers in me cast

Now, I wash my pious cloak with ruby-red wine,
    Knowing the destiny of eternity we cannot cast

Did Hafez's lucky break start from these very ruins?
    Where into the wine of the Magi, his eternal bounty, he cast.

Now the world will be more to my advantage, as the turns of time
    Have me serving the Master of the World, my die is cast.

COMMENTARY ON 2ND TRANSLATION

In this translation we explore love's intoxicating power and the surrender to divine destiny. The speaker is captivated by the beloved's beauty and charm, likening their eyebrow to a bow that aims to pierce their heart. The poem is filled with vivid imagery and metaphors, evoking the beauty of nature and the transformative power of love. Here Hafez explores love's transformative power. The speaker's journey from piety to abandon, from doubt to surrender, is a testament to the irresistible allure of love. The poem's rich imagery and passionate language create a vivid and unforgettable portrait of the human heart in the throes of love.

The opening verse sets the tone for the poem by highlighting the beloved's captivating allure. The curve of their eyebrow is compared to a bow, and the speaker feels helpless in the face of their charm.

The second verse explores the theme of love's predestined nature. The speaker acknowledges that love was not part of the original design of the world, but it has emerged as a powerful force that transcends time and space.

The third verse describes the mischievous nature of the beloved's eyes, which have the power to incite rebellion and unrest. The narcissus, a symbol of vanity and self-love, is used to illustrate the beloved's captivating beauty.

The fourth verse introduces the theme of intoxication and the abandonment of reason. The beloved's wine-induced behavior has set a fire in the tulip, a symbol of passion and desire.

The fifth verse recounts the speaker's own experience of intoxication and doubt. They wander through the meadow in a drunken stupor, unsure of their own feelings and desires.

The sixth and seventh verses describe the beauty of nature and the interconnectedness of all things. The violet's twisted locks are compared to the beloved's hair, and the morning breeze is seen as a messenger of love.

The eighth verse explores the theme of shame and regret. The speaker feels ashamed for attributing the beloved's beauty to their own face, and the jasmine, a symbol of purity and innocence, is used to represent the speaker's remorse.

The ninth verse marks a turning point in the poem. The speaker abandons their previous piety and embraces the pleasures of wine and music. The tavern-goers, symbols of revelry and abandon, have awakened a new desire within the speaker.

The tenth verse solidifies the speaker's transformation. They wash their pious cloak in wine, acknowledging that their destiny is intertwined with the intoxicating power of love.

The eleventh verse reflects on the speaker's past and the events that led them to this point. They wonder if their lucky break began with the ruins of their former life, where they first tasted the wine of the Magi, a symbol of divine wisdom and love.

The final verse expresses the speaker's newfound contentment with the world. The turns of time have led them to serve the Master of the world, a metaphor for the divine beloved, and this service has brought them a sense of peace and fulfillment.

CHAPTER 35
GHAZAL 17: LOVE'S FIERY EMBRACE

سینه از آتش دل، در غم جانانه بسوخت
آتشی بود در این خانه، که کاشانه بسوخت

تنم از واسطۀ دوری دلبر بگداخت
جانم از آتشِ مهرِ رخِ جانانه بسوخت

سوز دل بین که ز بس آتش اشکم، دل شمع
دوش بر من ز سر مِهر، چو پروانه بسوخت

آشنایی نه غریب است، که دلسوز من است

چون من از خویش برفتم، دل بیگانه بسوخت

خرقهٔ زهدِ مرا، آب خرابات ببرد
خانهٔ عقلِ مرا، آتش میخانه بسوخت

چون پیاله دلم از توبه که کردم بشکست
همچو لاله، جگرم بی می و خُمخانه بسوخت

ماجرا کم کن و بازآ که مرا مردم چشم
خرقه از سر به درآورد و به شکرانه بسوخت

ترک افسانه بگو حافظ و می نوش دمی
که نَخُفتیم شب و شمع به افسانه بسوخت

GHAZAL 17: LOVE'S FIERY EMBRACE

My heart, in longing for the beloved, is burning bright, in a fiery embrace
    There was a light in this dwelling, with the whole mansion alight in love's fiery embrace.

My body has wilted with the distance of the one who stole my heart,
    My soul, with the flame of her affectionate face, took flight in love's fiery embrace.

Behold my burning longing heart, from the heat of my tears, last night, in empathy
    the candle's heart burned for me, like a moth in love's fiery embrace.

My friends are not strangers to my longing, and in their empathy have burned for me before
    When I lose myself again, even a stranger's heart would be lit from my love's fiery embrace.

The wine water of the tavern washed away the piety of my ascetic robe,

And the house of my intellect was burned by the tavern's fiery embrace.

When the goblet of my repentance shattered into bits,
Like a tulip, without wine and flask, I would burn in love's fiery embrace.

My love, end this drama and come to me for the apple of my eye
Has disrobed, and in gratitude, has burned it in love's fiery embrace.

Cut the stories short, Hafez, and take a moment to sip this wine,
for we haven't slept and the candle is burning uselessly without love's fiery embrace.

COMMENTARY

This ghazal is a passionate exploration of love's consuming fire, as the speaker's heart and soul are ablaze with longing for the beloved. This intense emotion transforms their entire being, leading them to abandon reason and embrace the intoxicating power of love. Hafez evokes an expression of the transformative power of love through rich imagery and passionate language, creating a vivid and unforgettable portrait of the human heart in the throes of love.

Fire (آتش)

The opening verse sets the tone for the poem, with the speaker's heart burning brightly with sorrow for the beloved. This fire of love has engulfed the speaker's entire dwelling, consuming them completely. The second verse describes the physical and spiritual effects of this love. The speaker's body has withered away due to the distance from the beloved, while their soul has taken flight, drawn towards the beloved's radiant face. In the first two couplets, Hafez uses "fire" as a metaphor to describe the intense emotional pain and burning caused by separation from the beloved. This fire consumes both the heart (metaphorically) and the home, symbolizing complete devastation due to love.

Heartburn (سوز دل)

The third verse shifts the focus to the speaker's heart, which has become a candle consumed by the heat of their tears. This imagery of the candle and the moth reinforces the theme of self-sacrifice and the willingness to endure pain for the sake of love.

The third couplet talks about the "burning of the heart," likening the poet's emotional suffering to a candle surrounded by moths (his tears), burning in devotion and unrequited love.

Familiarity (آشنایی)

The fourth verse explores the paradox of familiarity and strangeness in love. The speaker finds comfort in the familiar presence of their own heart, yet they also feel a sense of estrangement from themselves when they stray from their true path.

In the fourth couplet, familiarity refers to the internal burning of the heart from personal transformation as Hafez moves away from his old self, indicating a deep existential change fueled by his emotional experiences.

Cloak of Piety (خرقهٔ زهد)

The fifth verse introduces the theme of intoxication and the abandonment of reason. The speaker's ascetic robe, a symbol of restraint and self-denial, is washed away by the waters of the tavern. The winehouse's fire consumes the speaker's rational abode, leaving them vulnerable to the intoxicating power of love.

The fifth couplet contrasts the spiritual and the worldly by describing how the "cloak of piety" is washed away by the tavern's waters, suggesting that spiritual pretensions are washed away, leading to a more genuine, albeit painful, spiritual renewal.

Cup (پیاله)

The sixth verse describes the shattering of the speaker's repentance, a symbol of their attempt to resist the temptations of love. The tulip, a traditional symbol of love and passion, is compared to the speaker's liver, which is wounded by the absence of wine and the beloved.

In the sixth couplet, Hafez breaks the cup of repentance, indicating a return to indulgence in worldly pleasures (symbolized by wine), which further burns his heart like a tulip — passionate and vibrant yet suffering.

Affair/Story (ماجرا)

The seventh verse expresses the speaker's exhaustion and their desire for a return to the beloved. Their vision has waned from the intensity of their longing, and they have discarded the robe of restraint in a gesture of surrender and gratitude.

The seventh couplet uses "affair" to symbolize the internal conflict and public consequences of Hafez's actions, as his spiritual cloak is metaphorically burned in a gesture of defiance or transformation.

Tale/Fable (افسانه)

The final verse brings the poem to a close with a call for silence and contemplation. The speaker urges Hafez to cease his stories and simply enjoy the present moment, acknowledging that they have stayed awake all night, consumed by the tales of love.

In the final couplet, "tale" represents the ephemeral nature of life and the fleeting pleasures it offers, as Hafez suggests abandoning tales to indulge in the momentary joy of wine, signifying an escape from the harsh realities of life through the metaphorical burning of the candle.

CHAPTER 36
GHAZAL 18: BLESSED BE TO YOU

ساقیا آمدنِ عید، مبارک بادت
وان مَواعید که کردی، مَرواد از یادت

در شگفتم که در این مدّتِ ایّامِ فراق
برگرفتی ز حریفان دل و دل میدادت

برسان بندگی دختر رَز، گو به درآی
که دَم و همّت ما کرد ز بند آزادت

شادی مجلسیان در قدم و مقدم توست

جای غم باد، مَر آن دل، که نخواهد شادت

شکر ایزد که ز تاراجِ خزان رخنه نیافت
بوستانِ سمن و سرو و گل و شمشادت

چشمِ بد دور کز آن تفرقه‌ات بازآورد
طالعِ ناموَر و دولتِ مادرزادت

حافظ از دست مده دولتِ این کشتیِ نوح
ور نه طوفانِ حوادث بِبَرَد بُنیادت

GHAZAL 18: BLESSED BE TO YOU

O Saghi, the coming of the New Year, of Eid, blessed be to you,
   May your promises not fade from your memory, may they be, blessed for you .

I wonder how, in these days of separation, you have captivated hearts
   of companions and freely given your own, blessings be to you.

Send word that the daughter of the vine is in bondage, ask her to free herself,
   for all our toil and effort have been to free you, blessings onto you.

The joy of the assembly lies in your steps and approach,
   May sorrow be for that heart, which does not wish you joy, blessed be to you.

Thanks be to God, that the ravages of autumn did not breach
   your garden of jasmine, cypress, rose, and boxwood, blessings be to you.

May the evil eye that brought separation, be forever distant,

May your fate and fortune be transformed, blessings onto you.

Hafez, do not relinquish the fortune of this Noah's ark,
   lest the storm of events tear down your foundation, blessings onto you.

COMMENTARY

This ghazal is another heartfelt expression of love, longing, and well-wishes on the occasion of Eid – the New Year. The speaker addresses the beloved as "cupbearer," a traditional symbol of the one who serves wine and brings joy to others. The speaker's heartfelt wishes for the beloved's happiness and well-being resonate deeply with the reader, leaving a lasting impression of the power of love to transcend time and distance.

Celebration of Eid (ساقیا آمدنِ عید، مبارک بادت)

The first couplet celebrates the arrival of Eid, a festive time, wishing joy and reminding of promises made, emphasizing the importance of remembering and cherishing commitments during times of celebration. This sets the tone for the poem by expressing the speaker's desire for the beloved's happiness and well-being. The speaker wishes for the beloved's promises to be fulfilled and their memory to remain strong. The repetition of "blessings be to you" emphasizes the speaker's sincere and heartfelt wishes.

Wonder of Separation (در شکفتم که در این مدّتِ ایّامِ فراق)

In this couplet, Hafez expresses amazement at how, despite the long period of separation, the beloved has managed to captivate hearts and continue to give away their heart generously to others. This expresses the speaker's wonder at the beloved's ability to captivate hearts even in times of separation. The beloved is portrayed as a generous and loving figure who freely gives their own heart to others.

Servitude of the Daughter of Riz (برسان بندگیِ دختر رَز، گو به درآی)

Hafez invokes the notion of servitude, possibly metaphorical, encouraging boldness and freedom from constraints, suggesting an overcoming or liberation from servile conditions.

The third verse introduces the metaphor of the "daughter of the vine," representing wine and its intoxicating power. The speaker encourages the beloved to free themselves from the bondage of worldly concerns and to embrace the joy of love.

Joy of the Gathering (شادی مجلسیان در قدم و مقدم توست)

The fourth verse celebrates the beloved's presence and the joy it brings to others. The speaker wishes sorrow upon those who do not share in the joy of the beloved's company.

This couplet highlights the joy and happiness that the arrival of the beloved brings to a gathering, banishing sorrow and desiring happiness for those who are reluctant to embrace joy.

Gratitude to God (شکر ایزد که ز تاراجِ خزان رخنه نیافت)

The fifth verse expresses gratitude for the beloved's resilience and strength in the face of adversity. The beloved's garden, a symbol of their beauty and inner peace, has remained untouched by the ravages of time.

Hafez expresses gratitude that the garden of life, filled with jasmine, cypress, roses, and evergreens, remains untouched by the devastation typically brought by autumn, symbolizing resilience and preservation of beauty.

Protection from Evil Eye (چشم بد دور کز آن تفرقه‌ات بازآورد)

The sixth verse expresses the speaker's hope for the beloved's future happiness and success. The speaker wishes for the evil eye of separation to be removed and for the beloved's fate to be transformed.

This couplet seeks protection against the evil eye that might cause division, calling for a fortunate destiny free from the negative influences that could disrupt unity and prosperity.

Fortunes of Noah's Ark (حافظ از دست مده دولت این کشتی نوح)

Hafez metaphorically references Noah's Ark as a symbol of salvation and survival, warning against losing this fortune to the storms of life's events, emphasizing the need to hold onto foundational strengths in the face of adversity.

The final verse offers a message of hope and encouragement. The speaker urges the beloved to hold onto the fortune of love and not to let the storms of life tear down their foundation.

CHAPTER 37
GHAZAL 19: WHERE IS THE BELOVED?

ای نسیم سحر آرامگهِ یار کجاست؟
منزلِ آن مَهِ عاشق‌کُشِ عیّار کجاست؟

شبِ تار است و رَه وادیِ اَیمَن در پیش

آتش طور کجا؟ موعد دیدار کجاست؟

هر که آمد به جهان نقش خرابی دارد
در خرابات بگویید که هشیار کجاست؟

آن کَس است اهلِ بشارت که اشارت داند
نکته‌ها هست بسی محرم اسرار کجاست؟

هر سرِ مویِ مرا با تو هزاران کار است
ما کجاییم و ملامتگر بی‌کار کجاست؟

باز پرسید ز گیسویِ شِکَن در شِکَنَش
کاین دل غمزده سرگشته، گرفتار کجاست؟

عقل دیوانه شد، آن سلسلهٔ مشکین کو؟
دل ز ما گوشه گرفت، ابروی دلدار کجاست؟

ساقی و مطرب و می جمله مهیاست ولی
عیش، بی‌یار مهیّا نشود، یار کجاست؟

حافظ از بادِ خزان، در چمنِ دهر مَرَنج
فکرِ معقول بفرما، گلِ بی‌خار کجاست؟

GHAZAL 19: WHERE IS THE BELOVED?

Saba, Fresh Breeze of Dawn, tell me, where is my Beloved? Where?
  Where is the home of that moon, that slayer of lovers? Where?

Traveling on this dark night with a clear path to safety that lies ahead,
  Where is the fire of Mount Sinai? Where is the appointed meeting? Where?

Everyone who comes into this world bears the mark of decay,
  Inside the tavern, tell me, where is the sober one? Where?

The one who understands subtle hints deserves the good news of union,
  There are many secrets, but where is the keeper of secrets?Where?

Each hair of mine has thousands of things to do with you,
  Look where we are, and where the idle critic is – where!

Again, ask then, of those tresses — full of twists and turns,
  Where is the tormented, ensnared heart to be found? Where?

Intellect has gone completely mad, where are those black chain-like tresses?

    The heart is suling in a corner, where are the beloved's brows? Where?

The cupbearer, the musician, and the wine, all are ready but

    Joy, without the beloved, is not possible, where is the beloved? Where?

Hafez, do not grieve over the autumn wind in the garden of time,

    Contemplate the feasible, where is the rose without thorns? Where?

COMMENTARY

This translation of Hafez's ghazal tries to capture the essence of longing, yearning, and the search for the divine Beloved. The poem employs a repeated question, "Where?", to emphasize the speaker's desperate quest for union with the Beloved.

The poem opens with an invocation to Saba, the fresh breeze of dawn, to reveal the whereabouts of the Beloved. This sets the tone for the rest of the poem, as the speaker continues to inquire about the location of the Beloved, comparing them to the moon and the fire of Mount Sinai. The moon, a symbol of beauty and unattainable love, is also described as a "slayer of lovers," highlighting the pain and longing associated with love.

The second verse introduces the theme of mortality and the transitory nature of life. The speaker acknowledges the inevitability of decay and wonders where one can find solace and sobriety in a world marked by impermanence. The tavern, often a symbol of worldly distractions and fleeting pleasures, is contrasted with the sober one, who may represent spiritual enlightenment or detachment from worldly concerns.

In the third verse, the speaker alludes to the importance of understanding subtle hints and hidden meanings in order to attain union with the Beloved. The emphasis on secrets and the keeper of secrets suggests that the path to divine love is not easily accessible and requires a deeper understanding of mystical knowledge.

The fourth verse shifts the focus to the speaker's personal connection with the Beloved. The speaker's hair, a symbol of their being, is intricately intertwined with the Beloved, highlighting the intimacy and interconnectedness of their relationship. The idle critic, who may represent those who lack understanding or appreciation for the speaker's love, is dismissed as irrelevant.

The fifth and sixth verses continue to explore the theme of longing and the speaker's tormented heart. The tresses, full of twists and turns, may symbolize the complexities of love and the challenges faced in the pursuit of the Beloved. The ensnared heart represents the speaker's captivity to love and their yearning for union.

The seventh and eighth verses express the speaker's frustration and despair. Intellect, which may represent rational thought and logic, has become overwhelmed by the intensity of love. The speaker's heart is sulking, unable to find solace without the Beloved's presence.

The ninth verse paints a scene of anticipation and preparation. The cupbearer, musician, and wine are all present, yet true joy is unattainable without the Beloved. This emphasizes the central role of the Beloved in bringing fulfillment and happiness.

The final verse offers a message of hope and acceptance. Hafez advises against grieving over the fleeting nature of time and encourages contemplation of the feasible. The rose without thorns, a symbol of perfection and unattainable beauty, is used to illustrate the idea that even in the face of loss and imperfection, there is still the possibility for beauty and joy.

This ghazal is a powerful and evocative exploration of love, longing, and the search for the divine. The poem's repeated questions, vivid imagery, and profound insights offer a timeless message of hope and resilience in the face of life's challenges.

Inquiry of the Beloved's Resting Place (ای نسیم سحر آرامگهِ یار کجـاست؟)

The ghazal opens with a question to the morning breeze about the location of the beloved's resting place, setting a tone of longing and search for the beloved.

The Dark Night and Safe Valley (شبِ تار است و رَه وادیِ اَیمَن در پیش)
Hafez contrasts the darkness of the night with the anticipated safety of the valley, metaphorically questioning the whereabouts of divine illumination and the appointed time of spiritual meeting.

Worldly Ruin and Awareness (هر که آمد به جهانِ نقش خرابی دارد)
This couplet reflects on the inherent decay in worldly existence and queries the state of awareness among those dwelling in ruin, symbolizing spiritual dilapidation.

Realm of the Enlightened (آن کَس است اهلِ بشارت که اشارت داند)
Hafez speaks of those enlightened who understand subtle hints, asking where the truly initiated, those privy to divine secrets, are located.

Multitude of Tasks (هر سرِ مویِ مرا با تو هزاران کار است)
This line describes the poet's overwhelming engagement with the beloved, contrasting his preoccupation with the idleness of critics.

Tangled Hair and Troubled Heart (باز پرسید ز کیسویِ شِکَن در شِکَنَش)
Hafez uses the metaphor of tangled hair to express the complexity of his troubled heart, questioning the whereabouts of his ensnared and distressed heart.

Madness of Reason (عقل دیوانه شد، آن سلسلهٔ مشکین کو؟)
The poet describes reason as becoming mad, searching for the dark chains (likely referring to the beloved's hair), questioning where the beloved's captivating features are that led to this madness.

Necessity of Companionship (ساقی و مطرب و می جمله مهیاست ولی)
Despite the readiness of the cupbearer, musician, and wine, Hafez points out the futility of pleasure without the beloved, emphasizing the essential nature of companionship for true joy.

Endurance in the Face of Change (حافظ از بادِ خزان، در چمنِ دهر مَرَنج)
The final couplet advises not to sorrow over the autumn winds in the garden of time, encouraging rational contemplation of the impermanent, questioning the existence of a thornless rose.

CHAPTER 38
GHAZAL 20: IN THIS FLEETING MOMENT

روزه یک سو شد و عید آمد و دل‌ها برخاست
می ز خُمخانه به جوش آمد و می‌باید خواست

نوبهٔ زهدفروشانِ گران جان بگذشت
وقتِ رندی و طرب کردن رندان پیداست

چه ملامت بود آن را که چنین باده خورَد؟
این چه عیب است بدین بی‌خردی، وین چه خطاست؟

باده نوشی که در او روی و ریایی نَبُوَد

بهتر از زهدفروشی، که در او روی و ریاست

ما نه رندان ریاییم و حریفان نفاق
آن که او عالِم سِرّ است، بدین حال گواست

فرض ایزد بگزاریم و به کس بد نکنیم
وان چه گویند روا نیست، نگوییم رواست

چه شود گر من و تو چند قدح باده خوریم؟
باده از خون رَزان است، نه از خون شماست

این چه عیب است کز آن عیب خلل خواهد بود
ور بُوَد نیز چه شد؟ مردم بی‌عیب کجاست

GHAZAL 20: IN THIS FLEETING MOMENT

The fast is done, *Eid* has come, our hearts rise,
    From the tavern, wine flows, now it's time for our prize.

The time of pious sellers has passed,
    It's the hour of joy for those who are wise.

What blame is there for one who drinks a cup this way?
    What fault is there in this folly — where the reprise?

To drink without show and hypocrisy is better
    than peddling a piety that is masked in lies.

We are not the Rends of hypocrisy, nor are we false friends,
    The one who is the Knower of Secrets can vouch for us.

So fulfill God's duty, and bring harm to no-one ,
    And that which is not to be done, we don't condone in disguise.

What harm if we drink a few cups?
    Wine is from grapes, not from your guise.

This fault causes no real harm,
    Who among men without flaws lies?

Hafez, cease questioning, just drink a moment,
    In the face of fate, no 'why' replies.

COMMENTARY

This ghazal captures the transition from fasting to celebration, emphasizing the importance of sincerity and balance in life. Each couplet highlights themes of joy, sincerity, and the rejection of hypocrisy.

In the first couplet, "روزه" (fasting), Hafez marks the end of fasting and the arrival of a festival, lifting everyone's spirits. The bubbling wine symbolizes the excitement and joy that accompany this festive time, urging people to embrace the moment.

The second couplet, "زهدفروشان" (ascetics), contrasts the burdensome period of asceticism with the present moment of revelry. Hafez suggests that the time of heavy-hearted piety has passed, and now it's time for merriment and carefree enjoyment.

In the third couplet, "ملامت" (blame), Hafez questions the criticism directed at those who indulge in wine. He argues that there is no fault in such folly and challenges the notion that drinking wine is a grievous error.

The fourth couplet, "ریایی" (hypocrisy), extols the virtues of sincere wine drinking over hypocritical piety. Hafez argues that genuine enjoyment without deceit is superior to outward displays of piety that are tainted with insincerity.

In the fifth couplet, "نفاق" (deceit), Hafez distances himself and his companions from pretentious and deceitful behavior. He emphasizes that those who understand the divine secret are aware of the sincerity and honesty in their actions, even in their enjoyment of life.

The sixth couplet, "بد" (harm), reaffirms Hafez's commitment to following divine laws and causing no harm to others. He maintains that they do not endorse actions considered wrong by others, but neither do they condemn them.

In the seventh couplet, "قدح" (cup), Hafez questions why sharing a few cups of wine should be seen as problematic. He poetically states that the wine comes from the tears of lovers, not from the blood of foes, suggesting that it symbolizes love and not harm.

The final couplet, "عیب" (flaw), questions the nature of perceived flaws and defects. Hafez asserts that everyone has imperfections and challenges the idea that enjoying wine and pleasure is a significant defect. He concludes by asking who among us is without flaws, emphasizing the universal nature of human imperfection.

CHAPTER 39
GHAZAL 21: SO, ARISE

دل و دینم شد و دلبر به ملامت برخاست
گفت با ما منشین کز تو سلامت برخاست

که شنیدی که در این بزم دمی خوش بنشست
که نه در آخر صحبت به ندامت برخاست

شمع اگر زان لب خندان به زبان لافی زد
پیش عشاق تو شبها به غرامت برخاست

در چمن باد بهاری ز کنار گل و سرو

به هواداری آن عارض و قامت برخاست

مست بگذشتی و از خلوتیان ملکوت
به تماشای تو آشوب قیامت برخاست

پیش رفتار تو پا برنگرفت از خجلت
سرو سرکش که به ناز از قد و قامت برخاست

حافظ این خرقه بینداز مگر جان ببری
کاتش از خرقه سالوس و کرامت برخاست

GHAZAL 21: SO, ARISE

My heart and faith were lost, and the beloved rose in blame,
  She said, "Do not sit with us; safety has departed you."

Who has heard of one who sat happily in this gathering,
  Who did not, in the end, rise in regret, didn't you?

If the candle boasted of those laughing lips,
  Lovers faced nights filled with grief, like you.

In the garden, the spring breeze rose from the rose and cypress,
  To show its devotion to that face and stature, like you.

You passed by the celestial beings, intoxicated, and
  the chaos of the day of judgement ensued at the sight of you.

In your presence, the proud and renegade cypress did not even
  lift its foot, chagrined of the grace and stature of yours.

Hafez, cast off this robe, if you wish to save your soul, for the
  fire of hypocrisy exudes from cloaks of false piety, like yours.

———

My heart and faith were lost, the beloved, in implication,
said, "Sit with us no longer; for your wholesomeness has gone.
Arise."

Who has heard of anyone who sat happily in that gathering,
And who did not, in the end, depart regretfully? So Arise.

If the candle dared to boast of the beloved's smiling lips, it was
condemned to spend nights burning and weeping before lovers. So
arise.

In the garden, the spring breeze rose from the rose and cypress,
to show its devotion to that face and stature, like you — arise.

You passed by the celestial beings, intoxicated, and thus
the chaos of the day of judgement ensued at the sight of you. Arise.

In your presence, the proud and renegade cypress did not even
dare lift its foot, chagrined by your grace and stature. So, arise.

Hafez, cast off this robe, if you wish to save your soul, for the
fire of hypocrisy exudes from cloaks of false piety — so arise

COMMENTARY

Hafez's ghazal captures the intense emotions and consequences of passionate love, examining themes of desire, regret, and the transient nature of beauty and companionship. Here is the commentary with a key word from each line:

In the first couplet, "ملامت" (reprimand), Hafez reveals that his heart and faith have been taken by his beloved, who then reproaches him. The beloved advises him not to sit with her, indicating that his presence disrupts her peace. This sets the tone for the turmoil and emotional upheaval in the realm of love.

In the second couplet, "ندامت" (regret), Hafez questions if anyone has ever sat joyfully in this gathering of love without eventually feeling regret. He suggests that companionship in love inevitably leads to remorse, highlighting the painful and fleeting nature of romantic relationships.

The third couplet, "شمع" (candle), uses the metaphor of a candle witnessing the beloved's laughing lips. The candle, if it could speak, would incite nightly passion among the lovers. This illustrates the beloved's captivating beauty and the powerful, almost mystical effect it has on those who admire her.

In the fourth couplet, "باد بهاری" (spring breeze), Hafez describes a spring breeze in the meadow, which moves from the side of the rose and cypress in admiration of the beloved's beauty and stature. This reflects how nature itself is moved by the beloved's grace, signifying the universal impact of her allure.

The fifth couplet, "مست" (intoxicated), portrays the beloved passing by in an intoxicated state, causing an uproar among the celestial beings who watch her. This suggests that her beauty is so extraordinary that it stirs even the divine beings, leading to a chaotic admiration comparable to the uproar of the Last Day.

In the sixth couplet, "سرو" (cypress), Hafez describes the tall cypress tree, a symbol of pride and beauty, standing still in humility before the beloved's walk. The cypress, known for its height and elegance, pales in comparison to the beloved's charm and grace, underscoring her unparalleled beauty.

The final couplet, "خرقه" (robe), advises Hafez to discard the robe of piety and honor. He suggests that the true essence of the soul can be found by letting go of pretenses and embracing the rawness of love. The robe, representing false piety, has only caused flames of desire and turmoil, implying that authenticity and vulnerability are the paths to spiritual and emotional fulfillment.

Hafez's ghazal masterfully blends metaphors and imagery to convey the intense experiences of love, beauty, and the inevitable regrets and transformations they bring. Each couplet delves deeper into the emotional and spiritual impact of love, highlighting the universal and timeless nature of these themes.

CHAPTER 40
GHAZAL 22: THERE WILL BE NO ERROR

چو بشنوی سخن اهل دل مگو که خطاست
سخن شناس نه‌ای جان من، خطا این جاست

سرم به دنیی و عقبی فرو نمی‌آید
تبارک الله از این فتنه‌ها که در سر ماست

در اندرون من خسته دل ندانم کیست
که من خموشم و او در فغان و در غوغاست

دلم ز پرده برون شد کجایی ای مطرب

بنال، هان که از این پرده کار ما به نواست

مرا به کار جهان هرگز التفات نبود
رخ تو در نظر من چنین خوشش آراست

نخفته‌ام ز خیالی که می‌پزد دل من
خمار صدشبه دارم شرابخانه کجاست

چنین که صومعه آلوده شد ز خون دلم
گرم به باده بشویید حق به دست شماست

از آن به دیر مغانم عزیز می‌دارند
که آتشی که نمیرد همیشه در دل ماست

چه ساز بود که در پرده می‌زد آن مطرب
که رفت عمر و هنوزم دماغ پُر ز هواست

ندای عشق تو دیشب در اندرون دادند
فضای سینه حافظ هنوز پر ز صداست

GHAZAL 22: THERE WILL BE NO ERROR

When you hear the words of the Fellowship of the Heart, don't say they are in error
For you are not, my dear, a knower of words, that is the error.

I don't bow to worldly allure nor the call of the Unmanifest realm, Blessed is the Divine!
May I remain free of these temptations that throng in our heads that leads to error.

Within me of weary heart, I don't know who it is that resides,
Amid its wails and clamor; I observe and remain silent, so it leads to no error.

My innermost heart came out, tore its veil; O minstrel, I need you to come, to sing out loud!
Beware, for there is no recourse for this Veil but to sing, so we don't fall into error.

I had never paid attention to the affairs of the world,
It was your face that adorned it for me with such beauty — am I in error?

I haven't slept, consumed by thoughts that brew in my heart,
    with a hangover of a hundred nights I still seek the wine-house in
error.

Since the cloister has been stained with the blood of my heart,
    If you want to wash me with wine, it's up to you, there will be no
error.

The reason I am cherished at the Magi's temple,
    is the undying fire that forever burns in my heart with no error.

What melody did that minstrel play from behind the veil, that
    even as my life has passed swiftly, I can still hear it with no error.

Last night, I was secretly informed of the call of your love, but
    the space in Hafez's chest still echoes in that melody with no error.

CHAPTER 41
COMMENTARY

HAFEZ'S ghazal deeply explores themes of spiritual longing, inner turmoil, and the ineffable nature of true love and understanding. Each couplet unveils the poet's profound reflections on the nature of the soul, the limitations of worldly pursuits, and the eternal quest for divine connection.

In the first couplet, "اهل دل" (heart's folk), Hafez advises not to dismiss the words of those who speak from the heart. He asserts that understanding deep, heartfelt speech requires a certain sensitivity and insight. The error lies in dismissing these profound truths without comprehending their depth.

The second couplet, "فتنه‌ها" (trials), reveals Hafez's refusal to bow to the allure of worldly or otherworldly promises. He marvels at the divine for placing such trials and complexities in their minds, indicating an inner conflict between worldly desires and spiritual aspirations.

In the third couplet, "فغان" (wails), Hafez speaks of an unknown presence within his weary heart that silently stays. Though he remains outwardly silent, this presence within him wails and causes inner turmoil, highlighting the intense, often unspoken, struggles of the soul.

The fourth couplet, "پرده" (veil), describes Hafez's heart escaping its veil, prompting a call to the minstrel. He urges the minstrel to sing out, as their task lies beyond these veils, in the realm of the melodic gong, symbolizing a deeper spiritual calling.

In the fifth couplet, "رخ تو" (your face), Hafez expresses his indifference to worldly matters, finding all his fulfillment in the vision of the beloved's face. This face, adorned in his vision, has made everything else seem insignificant.

The sixth couplet, "خمار صدشبه" (weight of a hundred nights), reveals Hafez's sleeplessness, haunted by a vision that stirs his heart. He carries the heavy burden of longing, seeking solace in the tavern's company, representing the search for spiritual or emotional relief.

The seventh couplet, "صومعه آلوده" (monastery stained), reflects on how the monastery is stained with the blood of his heart. Hafez suggests washing it with wine, implying that sometimes righteousness and purification come from unexpected sources, like the tavern.

In the eighth couplet, "آتشی که نمیرد" (undying flame), Hafez explains why he is cherished in the tavern of wine-drinkers: an eternal flame burns within his heart. This undying flame symbolizes his unwavering passion and spiritual fervor, which the tavern-goers recognize and revere.

The ninth couplet, "دماغ پُر ز هوا" (mind's filled with its echoing song), speaks to the haunting effect of a minstrel's tune played behind the veil. Even as life passes, Hafez's mind remains filled with the echo of that song, indicating the lasting impact of spiritual and emotional experiences.

In the final couplet, "ندای عشق" (love's call), Hafez recounts how the call of love echoed within him last night. His chest still resonates with that melodious call, signifying the profound and enduring nature of true love and spiritual awakening.

Hafez's ghazal eloquently captures the internal conflicts and spiritual aspirations of the soul. Through rich metaphors and poignant reflections, he explores the themes of love, inner turmoil, and the pursuit of divine connection, emphasizing the importance of understanding and embracing the deeper, often hidden, truths of existence.

CHAPTER 42
GHAZAL 23: IN EVERY BREATH I TAKE

خیالِ رویِ تو در هر طریق همره ماست
نسیمِ مویِ تو پیوندِ جانِ آگه ماست

به رغم مدعیانی که منع عشق کنند
جمالِ چهرهٔ تو حجت موجه ماست

ببین که سیب زنخدان تو چه می‌گوید
هزار یوسف مصری فتاده در چهِ ماست

اگر به زلف دراز تو دست ما نرسد

گناه بخت پریشان و دست کوته ماست

به حاجبِ درِ خلوت سرایِ خاص بگو
فُلان ز گوشه نشینانِ خاکِ درگهِ ماست

به صورت از نظر ما اگر چه محجوب است
همیشه در نظرِ خاطرِ مرفهِ ماست

اگر به سالی حافظ دری زند بگشای
که سال‌هاست که مشتاق روی چون مه ماست

GHAZAL 23: IN EVERY BREATH I TAKE

A more lyrical interpretation and translation

Your face's vision, in every path, walks side by side, in every breath I take,
    The breeze of your hair, is the anchor of the awakened soul, in every breath I take.

Despite the naysayers who decry and deny the very state of love,
    Your face's beauty stands as my most valid argument, in every breath I take.

See what the apple of your cheek says, a thousand Josephs
    of Egypt lie in that well of our chin, in every breath I take.

If to your long tresses our hands cannot partake, you can blame
    My pitiful fate and short reach but I still seek you, in every breath I take.

To the guard of the Place of Silent remembrance, that special place, do relate,

That I am but one of the corner sitters, of your court, with every breath I take.

Though your form from our gaze might be hidden and opaque,
Always in the refined thought's eye, you partake, in every breath I take.

If once in a year, to Hafez, you grant an entrance stake,
For years, I have longed for a face as luminous as the moon's wake, in every breath I take.

GHAZAL 23: ALWAYS WITH US — ALTERNATIVE TRANSLATION

ALWAYS WITH US

The thought of your face accompanies us on every path—*always with us*
   The breeze through your hair binds our awakened souls—*always with us.*

Despite those rivals who seem to have forbade this love,
   The beauty of your face is our undeniable proof—*always with us.*

Listen to that silent message of your dimpled chin which says:
   A thousand Josephs have fallen into this well — you are *always with us.*

If our hands are not able to reach your long tresses,
   Blame our troubled fate and short reach— but you are *always with us.*

Tell the chamberlain of that private court of silence,
   So-and-so is a recluse who resides in the dust of your threshold—*always with us.*

Though you may be hidden from our sight,
    You are ever-present in our sight and give our heart's ease—*always with us.*

If Hafez should knock at your door once a year, open it, for he
    has long been yearning for your shining face—though you are *always with us.*

CHAPTER 43
COMMENTARY

THIS GHAZAL IS another profound exploration of love, longing, and spiritual devotion. Each couplet reflects his deep emotional connection to the beloved, the challenges posed by critics, and the enduring nature of his affection.

In the first couplet, "خیالِ رویِ تو" (the thought of your face), Hafez declares that the thought of the beloved's face accompanies him in every path he takes. The gentle breeze that carries the scent of the beloved's hair binds his soul to her presence. This imagery conveys the omnipresence of the beloved in his thoughts and the deep, spiritual connection he feels.

In the second couplet, "جمالِ چهرهٔ تو" (the beauty of your face), Hafez addresses those who criticize and forbid love. He asserts that the beauty of the beloved's face is his most compelling argument and justification for his love. This indicates that the beloved's beauty transcends societal norms and criticisms, serving as a divine and irrefutable proof of his feelings.

The third couplet, "سیب زنخدان" (the dimple on your chin), uses the metaphor of the dimple on the beloved's chin to convey a deeper meaning. Hafez suggests that this dimple speaks of countless Josephs (a symbol of beauty) falling into the well of his love. This metaphor highlights the irresistible allure of the beloved and the depth of his infatuation, suggesting that many have been captivated and lost in her beauty.

In the fourth couplet, "زلف دراز" (long hair), Hafez laments that his hand cannot reach the beloved's long hair. He attributes this to his unfortunate destiny and his short reach, symbolizing the obstacles and limitations he faces in attaining his desires. This couplet speaks to the themes of longing and the pain of unattainable love.

The fifth couplet, "حاجب در خلوت سرای خاص" (the chamberlain of the private court), instructs the chamberlain to recognize that a certain reclusive person belongs to their circle. This suggests that even those who are withdrawn and humble have a place in the intimate court of the beloved, emphasizing the inclusivity and universal nature of love and devotion.

In the sixth couplet, "به صورت از نظر ما اگر چه محجوب است" (though veiled from our sight in form), Hafez acknowledges that while the beloved may be physically veiled from his sight, she remains ever-present in his thoughts. This illustrates the enduring nature of his love, which transcends physical presence and remains strong in his heart and mind.

The final couplet, "حافظ دری زند بگشای" (if Hafez knocks, open the door), is a plea for the beloved to open the door if he knocks, even if only once in a year. Hafez expresses his long-standing desire and yearning to see the beloved's moon-like face, indicating that his love and longing have persisted for many years. This couplet encapsulates the themes of patience, hope, and enduring love.

It beautifully weaves themes of love, longing, and spiritual devotion through rich imagery and metaphors. Each couplet reflects his deep emotional connection to the beloved, the challenges posed by societal norms and critics, and the timeless nature of his affection. This ghazal stands as a testament to the enduring power of love and the spiritual depth of Hafez's poetry.

CHAPTER 44
GHAZAL 24: THE POWER OF LOVE

مطلب طاعت و پیمان و صلاح از منِ مست

که به پیمانه کشی شهره شدم روز الست

من همان دم که وضو ساختم از چشمه عشق

چارتکبیر زدم یکسره بر هر چه که هست

می بده تا دهمت آگهی از سِرِّ قضا

که به رویِ که شدم عاشق و از بوی که مست

کمر کوه کم است از کمر مور این جا

نا امید از در رحمت مشو ای باده پرست

به جز آن نرگس مستانه که چشمش مَرِساد
زیر این طارِم فیروزه کسی خوش ننشست

جان فدای دهنش باد که در باغ نظر
چمن آرای جهان خوشتر از این غنچه نبست

حافظ از دولت عشق تو سلیمانی شد
یعنی از وصل تواش نیست به جز باد به دست

GHAZAL 24: THE POWER OF LOVE

Don't expect my obedience, covenant, or rectitude, for I am drunk, by the power of love

I am famed for carrying cups till the *Day of Alast*, with the power of love

The moment I purified myself at the fountain of love,
    I incanted 'God is the greatest' on all that exists, with the power of love

Give me wine, that I may reveal to you the secrets of destiny, to tell
    with whose face I fell in love, by whose scent I was intoxicated, through the power of love

Here, a mountain's waist is less than an ant's, do not despair
    at the door of Hope, O worshiper of wine, for the power of love

Except for that drunken iris whose glance would strike down,
    Under this turquoise dome, no one else sat content, but through the power of love

May my soul be sacrificed for that mouth, in the garden of Insights,
    No gardener of the world has bloomed a sweeter bud, with the power of love

Through the power of Your love, Hafez, became Solomon-like,
    Meaning, from this union, he can hold none other than the wind in hand, with the power of love

GHAZAL 24: THE POWER OF LOVE: ALTERNATIVE TRANSLATION

From this drunkard, seek not piety or vows, the power of love,
  Known for my pledges made on the Day of Alast, the power of love.

In that moment, I washed in the spring of affection, bathed in devotion,
  And declared God's greatness, over all that is, the power of love.

Pour the wine, let me reveal the secret of fate, unveiled through clarity,
  By whose face I'm smitten, by whose scent I'm drunk, the power of love.

Where mountains are lesser than an ant's waist, amidst the vast divine,
  Despair not at mercy's gate, you who worships wine, the power of love.

Save for that tipsy iris, whose glance can fell, a look that captivates,
  Under this azure vault, none other finds joy, the power of love.

For her lips alone, my soul is sacrificed, to the altar of her beauty,

No gardener of worlds has bound a lovelier bud, the power of love.

Through your love's kingdom, Hafez turned Solomon, ruler of hearts,
From your embrace, all he grasps is the wind, the power of love.

COMMENTARY

The "Day of *Alast*" (or "*Yawm al-Alast*") is a significant concept within Sufi thought, derived from the Qur'an, specifically the verse (7:172) which alludes to a primordial covenant or event that took place before the creation of the physical world.

The term "*Alast*" comes from the phrase in the Qur'an: "*Alastu bi rabbikum?*" which translates as "Am I not your Lord?" To which the souls of all human beings responded: "*Bala, shahidna*" meaning "Yes, we bear witness."

In Sufi interpretation, the Day of *Alast* represents the *eternal covenant that every soul made with God before descending into the material world*.

This moment signifies the innate knowledge and recognition every soul has of its Creator. It embodies the idea that the essence of belief and the recognition of God is imprinted within the soul of every human being.

The Day of Alast also serves as a reminder of the soul's original purity and its deep connection with the Divine. The forgetfulness, or lack consideration or "ghaflah" of this primal covenant is seen as a reason for the soul's journey in the physical world, striving to return and reconnect with the Divine.

Many Sufi teachings emphasize the importance of remembering this original covenant, as it is foundational to understanding one's purpose in life and the innate longing to return to a state of union with God. It underscores the idea that the human soul inherently recognizes and yearns for its Creator, even if it becomes distracted or forgetful due to the challenges and illusions of the worldly life.

SOLOMON AND THE WIND

Solomon, known as *Sulaiman* in Islamic/Persian tradition, is one of the most fascinating figures both in the Quran and Biblical texts, with several miraculous abilities attributed to him. His control over the wind is a particularly celebrated aspect, symbolizing divine favor and authority. Here's a recount of the tales and traditions concerning Solomon and his command over the wind:

Historic Perspectives and Islamic Tradition

1. Transportation and Speed: The Quran states that Solomon had control over the wind, which he could manipulate to serve his needs for transportation. It would blow gently at his command and could travel the distance equivalent to a month's journey in both the morning and the afternoon. This allowed him to cover vast distances quickly, effectively shrinking the world in terms of travel time.
2. Spiritual Reference: In Surah Sawd (38:36), it is mentioned, *"And to Solomon [We subjected] the wind, blowing forcefully, proceeding by his command toward the land which We had blessed. And We are ever, of all things, Knowing."*
3. Material Use: Solomon also used the wind to support his military campaigns. It helped in deploying troops swiftly across battlefields and territories, providing strategic advantages over his enemies.

Biblical Tradition

1. General Mention: While the Hebrew Bible does not explicitly mention Solomon's control over the wind like the Quran, his wisdom and the descriptions of his reign often imply a mastery over nature and the natural order, which aligns with the broader themes of his divine right and kingly status.

Folklore and Later Interpretations

1. Architectural Marvels: Jewish, Christian, and Islamic traditions suggest that Solomon used his control over the wind and his command of demons and jinn to build the Temple in Jerusalem and other magnificent structures. These tales often highlight his ability to harness the natural and supernatural world to manifest his visions.
2. Spiritual Symbolism: In mystical and esoteric traditions, such as Sufism, Solomon's control over the wind is seen as a metaphor for spiritual mastery over the self and the natural world. This control symbolizes the ability to navigate the spiritual landscape, directing the 'winds' of divine grace to achieve profound spiritual insights and states.
3. Literary Uses: Poets and writers have often used Solomon's control over the wind as a symbol of ultimate power and divine favor, as seen in Hafez's poetry. This symbolic use underscores the theme that true spiritual power transcends physical possessions and worldly authority.

Solomon's ability to control the wind, therefore, encapsulates various themes across different traditions—ranging from literal and historical interpretations about his reign and capabilities to more metaphorical and spiritual interpretations about his wisdom and spiritual stature. In every tradition, his control over the wind serves to underline his unique standing as a figure of immense authority, both divinely ordained and spiritually profound.

DETAILED COMMENTARY

Hafez's ghazal delves deeply into the themes of love, fate, and spiritual transformation, each couplet highlighting a key aspect of his philosophical and mystical beliefs. Here is a detailed commentary with a key phrase or term from each line:

In the first couplet, "منِ مست" (the intoxicated one), Hafez sets the tone by rejecting conventional expectations of piety from someone who is intoxicated by love and divine ecstasy. He emphasizes that his devotion transcends traditional religious practices and enters the realm of mystical intoxication.

The second couplet, "وضو ساختم از چشمه عشق" (ablution from the spring of love), describes a transformative spiritual experience. Hafez declares that when he purified himself with the waters of love, he renounced all worldly attachments with the proclamation of "الله اکبر" (God is the Greatest) four times, signifying his complete submission to divine love.

In the third couplet, "سرِّ قضا" (secrets of fate), Hafez uses wine as a metaphor for divine knowledge. He suggests that through the mystical experience of wine-drinking, he can reveal the secrets of fate and destiny, symbolizing the deep connection between love, beauty, and spiritual enlightenment.

The fourth couplet, "کمر مور" (the ant's waist), highlights the vastness of divine mercy. Hafez reassures the wine-worshipper not to despair, suggesting that even the smallest beings, like an ant, can find grace and strength in the presence of the divine.

In the fifth couplet, "نرکس مستانه" (drunken narcissus), Hafez elevates the beloved's eye above all others. The beloved's eye, likened to a narcissus, symbolizes the unique and incomparable nature of the beloved's gaze, which captivates and enchants all who behold it.

The sixth couplet, "جان فدای دهنش" (may my soul be sacrificed for her mouth), praises the beloved's lips, comparing them to the most beautiful and cherished bud in the garden of perception. Hafez expresses his willingness to sacrifice his soul for the beloved's mouth, highlighting the profound impact of her beauty.

In the final couplet, "دولت عشق تو سلیمانی" (the fortune of your love), Hafez likens himself to King Solomon, implying that the union with the beloved has granted him immense spiritual wealth and insight. Despite this exalted state, he concludes that his only true possession remains the wind, symbolizing the ephemeral nature of worldly achievements compared to divine love.

Here we see an intricate weaving of themes of spiritual transformation, the power of love, and the pursuit of divine beauty. Each key phrase encapsulates the essence of the mystical journey, emphasizing that true enlightenment is sought through the intoxicating power of love and divine connection.

CHAPTER 45
GHAZAL 25: THE NIGHTINGALE WAS DRUNK

شکفته شد گل حَمرا و گشت بلبل مست
صلایِ سرخوشی، ای صوفیان باده پرست

اساس توبه که در محکمی چو سنگ نمود
ببین که جام زُجاجی چه طُرفه‌اش بشکست

بیار باده که در بارگاه استغنا
چه پاسبان و چه سلطان، چه هوشیار و چه مست

از این رباط دوبَر، چون ضرورت است رَحیل

رواق و طاقِ معیشت، چه سربلند و چه پست

مقام عیش میسر نمی‌شود بی‌رنج
بلی به حکم بلا بسته‌اند عهد الست

به هست و نیست مرنجان ضمیر و خوش می‌باش
که نیستی است سرانجام هر کمال که هست

شکوه آصفی و اسب باد و منطق طیر
به باد رفت و از او خواجه هیچ طَرف نبست

به بال و پَر مرو از ره که تیر پرتابی
هوا گرفت زمانی، ولی به خاک نشست

زبان کلکِ تو حافظ چه شکر آن گوید
که گفتهٔ سخنت می‌برند دست به دست

GHAZAL 25: THE NIGHTINGALE WAS DRUNK

The rose unfolds, the nightingale intoxicated in song,
    In dance and whirl, Sufis understand wine's delight.

Vows once deemed unyielding, now appear so wrong,
    A fragile glass reveals a world, so slight in wine's delight.

Pour the wine, in courts where material treasures throng,
    Guard or monarch, inebriated or in the light, all seek wine's delight.

This transient abode, with departure foregone,
    Towers of existence, irrespective of their plight, fade into wine's delight.

Joy's place is entwined with trials, enduring and long,
    By divine decree, in struggles and despite, we're bound by wine's delight.

Existence or the abyss, to both we belong,
    End of every perfection is nonexistence, a sight in wine's delight.

Legends of yore, magic tales and ancient song,

With time, they vanish, leaving no trace or right, save for wine's delight.

Trust not mere wings, for even arrows once strong,
Soared for a while, but to the earth took flight, grounded by wine's delight.

Your eloquence, oh Hafez, resounds and prolongs,
Words passed from hand to hand, echoing the might of wine's delight.

GHAZAL 25: ALTERNATIVE – THE NIGHTINGALE WAS DRUNK

The red rose has bloomed, and the nightingale sings—*drunk on beauty*,
 A call to joy echoes, O wine-loving Sufis—*drunk on beauty*.

Repentance seemed as solid as stone,
 But a fragile glass in your hand shattered—*drunk on faith*.

Bring forth the wine, for in this realm,
 The king and the beggar stand alike—*drunk on freedom*.

Since we must depart from this fleeting world,
 What does it matter if our life's arch is high or low—*drunk on fate*?

The pleasure of life does not come without pain,
 The eternal covenant was sealed—*drunk on love*.

Do not fret over existence or non-existence, find peace,
 For all that exists will end in nothingness—*drunk on truth*.

The glory of kings, the speed of the wind, the language of birds,
 All of it vanished, leaving us—*drunk on loss*.

Do not rely on wings to carry you, for an arrow shot,
   Though it soars, it will fall—*drunk on pride.*

How can your pen, O Hafez, express gratitude,
   When your words, passed hand to hand, leave all—*drunk on wisdom?*

GHAZAL 25: ALTERNATIVE TRANSLATION

The red rose has bloomed and the nightingale is drunk,
  O the joy of ecstasy, O Sufis who worship wine!

The foundation of repentance, though as solid as stone it seemed,
  See how it marvelously shattered by the glass cup.

Bring wine, for in the court of sufficiency,
  Whether guard or king, whether sober or drunk.

From this transient abode, as departure is necessary,
  The arches and vaults of living, high or low.

The station of pleasure is not achieved without struggle,
  Indeed, by the decree of affliction, the covenant of 'Alast' is bound.

Let not existence or non-existence grieve your soul, and be merry,
  For nonexistence is ultimately the end of every perfection that
exists.

The glory of Asif, the wind-borne horse, and the language of birds,

All went with the wind, and from it, the master made no profit.

Do not rely on wings and feathers for the journey, for like a shot arrow,
　　It soared for a while, but ultimately rested on the ground.

How sweetly does your pen speak, Hafez,
　　Your words are passed hand to hand.

COMMENTARY

This ghazal captures profound themes of spiritual enlightenment, the transient nature of worldly pursuits, and the quest for divine connection. Each couplet unfolds deeper insights and metaphors that convey his mystical and philosophical reflections.

In the first couplet, "بلبل مست" (intoxicated nightingale) represents the soul's ecstatic response to divine beauty. The blooming red rose symbolizes the manifestation of divine beauty, and the intoxicated nightingale emphasizes the joy and spiritual ecstasy experienced in its presence. The call to joy directed at the Sufis underscores the idea that true spiritual enlightenment comes through experiencing divine love and beauty.

In the second couplet, "جام زُجاجی" (glass goblet) symbolizes the fragile nature of human resolutions and repentance. Despite appearing solid, these resolutions can easily break under pressure. Hafez marvels at how the seemingly strong foundation of repentance shatters, highlighting human frailty and the need for divine grace for true steadfastness.

In the third couplet, "بارگاه استغنا" (court of divine indifference) represents a state where worldly distinctions and hierarchies become meaningless. Hafez suggests that in the realm of divine love and enlightenment, all earthly statuses and conditions are irrelevant, emphasizing that spiritual truth transcends material concerns.

In the fourth couplet, "رباط دودر" (two-door caravanserai) serves as a metaphor for the transient nature of life. Just as travelers must eventually leave a caravanserai, humans must depart from this world. This imagery emphasizes the futility of worldly status and achievements, as all will ultimately pass.

In the fifth couplet, "عهد الست" (primordial covenant) refers to the pre-eternal pact between God and humanity, suggesting that suffering is an inherent part of the human condition. Hafez implies that true joy and spiritual enlightenment come through enduring and overcoming afflictions, which are part of this divine agreement.

In the sixth couplet, "نیستی" (non-being) is the ultimate fate of all existence. Hafez advises finding contentment and not being troubled by the temporary nature of existence. He reflects on the concept of non-being as the end of all that exists, highlighting the importance of spiritual contentment.

In the seventh couplet, "باد" (wind) symbolizes the fleeting nature of worldly power and knowledge. Hafez references Asaf's grandeur, Solomon's wind-steed, and the speech of birds to point out that these accomplishments ultimately proved transient and unsubstantial, reinforcing the message that worldly achievements are ephemeral.

In the eighth couplet, "تیر پرتابی" (arrow) suggests that human efforts and ambitions, like an arrow, may soar briefly but will ultimately fall. Hafez counsels against relying solely on one's abilities and advocates for humility and reliance on divine guidance, recognizing the limitations of human endeavors.

In the ninth couplet, "كلک" (reed pen) symbolizes Hafez's means of expression. He reflects on the gratitude he feels for the widespread appreciation and sharing of his poetry. This concluding couplet highlights the power of poetry to transcend time and place, sharing the poet's insights and emotions with future generations.

The rich imagery and philosophical reflections of this poem underscores the transient nature of worldly pursuits, the importance of spiritual devotion, and the profound joy found in the divine. Each couplet builds upon these themes, creating a tapestry of mystical thought that *encourages the reader to look beyond the material world and seek deeper, spiritual fulfillment.*

COMMENTARY ON THE ALTERNATIVE TRANSLATION

The ghazal beautifully captures essential elements of Sufi thought, weaving together imagery of nature, the ephemeral nature of worldly structures, and the pursuit of divine ecstasy. The opening couplet sets the stage with the blossoming of a rose and the intoxication of a nightingale, symbols of natural beauty and spiritual intoxication respectively, reflecting the Sufi quest for divine love.

The broken foundation of repentance by a glass cup symbolizes the fragility of human resolutions in the face of divine intoxication. This idea suggests that divine love or the experience of spiritual ecstasy can shatter conventional commitments, drawing the mystic closer to a higher truth.

The third couplet introduces a democratic spiritual environment where worldly status (guard or king) and states of consciousness (sober or drunk) are equalized in the court of sufficiency, likely referring to the equalizing nature of divine presence or the spiritual realm where external distinctions lose their meaning.

The reference to the transient abode and its arches, high or low, points to the temporary nature of life and earthly distinctions. This is a call to focus on the eternal and not be overly concerned with temporal hierarchies.

The line about the covenant of 'Alast' (referring to the pre-eternal covenant mentioned in the Quran) bound by the decree of affliction, suggests that human souls are tested with difficulties to ultimately remember and return to their divine promise.

The dismissal of the ultimate significance of existence or non-existence reflects a profound Sufi philosophy of annihilation (fana) and subsistence (baqa) in God, where the end of all apparent perfections is nonexistence, leading to the true existence in the divine.

The mention of Asif (the wise minister of King Solomon with control over the wind), the wind-borne horse, and the language of birds alludes to the ephemeral nature of worldly powers and knowledge, which, despite their seeming grandeur, dissipate like the wind.

Finally, the caution against relying on one's own power (wings and feathers) and the sweetness of Hafez's pen underscore the themes of humility and the enduring impact of spiritual poetry.

Overall, the ghazal is a reflection on the transient nature of worldly life and the enduring pursuit of spiritual truth, emphasizing the importance of divine love and the realization of one's ultimate return to nonexistence, which paradoxically leads to true eternal existence.

CHAPTER 46
GHAZAL 26: WHY ARE YOU STILL ASLEEP?

زلف‌آشفته و خوی‌کرده و خندان‌لب و مست
پیرهن‌چاک و غزل‌خوان و صُراحی در دست

نرگسش عربده‌جویَ و لبش افسوس‌کنان
نیم شب دوش به بالین من آمد بنشست

سر فرا گوش من آورد به آواز حزین
گفت ای عاشق دیرینهٔ من خوابت هست؟

عاشقی را که چنین بادهٔ شبگیر دهند

کافر عشق بود گر نشود باده پرست

برو ای زاهد و بر دُردکشان خرده مگیر
که ندادند جز این تحفه به ما روز الست

آن چه او ریخت به پیمانهٔ ما نوشیدیم
اگر از خَمر بهشت است وگر بادهٔ مست

خندهٔ جامِ می و زلفِ گرهگیر نگار
ای بسا توبه که چون توبه حافظ بشکست

GHAZAL 26: WHY ARE YOU STILL ASLEEP?

Disheveled hair, soaked in perfume, with smiling lips and drunk, half-asleep
    Shirt torn, singing ghazals, a wine glass in hand, half-asleep.

Her narcissus eyes contentious, her lips smacking in regret,
    At midnight she came to my bedside and sat by me, half-asleep.

She brought her mouth close to my ear with a sad voice,
    Whispered, "My ancient lover, why are you still asleep?"

Lovers who receive such early morning wine, to love
    would be faithless if they are not intoxicated, so never asleep.

Go, O ascetic, and do not fault the wine drinkers,
    For this gift was given to us on the day of the covenant, while asleep.

Whatever she poured into our cup, we drank,
    Whether it was heavenly wine or intoxicating wine, almost asleep.

The laughter of the wine cup and the lover's tangled curls,
    How many vows like Hafez's have been broken, seeming asleep.

COMMENTARY

Here we have a portrayal of the enchanting yet tumultuous experience and interplay of love and spiritual intoxication. Starting with the allure of the beloved, the paradoxes of love, and the poet's reflections on divine and earthly intoxication.

In the first couplet, "زلف‌آشفته و خوی‌کرده و خندان‌لب و مست" (Disheveled hair, sweat-soaked, smiling lips, and intoxicated), our poet paints a picture of the beloved with disheveled hair, sweat-soaked skin, smiling lips, and a state of intoxication. The beloved appears carefree and absorbed in the moment, holding a wine flask and singing ghazals, a scene that captures the essence of both physical beauty and a spirit unbound by societal norms.

In the second couplet, "نرگسش عربده‌جوی و لبش افسوس‌کنان" (Her narcissus eyes quarrelsome and her lips regretful), the beloved, with eyes like quarrelsome narcissus flowers and regretful lips, comes to the narrator's bedside at midnight. This arrival, blending aggressive beauty and tender regret, emphasizes the unpredictable and complex nature of love.

In the third couplet, "سر فرا کوش من آورد به آواز حزین" (She brought her head close to my ear with a sorrowful voice), the beloved leans in and speaks sorrowfully, asking the narrator if he is asleep. This intimate moment highlights the depth of their connection and the beloved's awareness of Hafez's sleepless longing and pain.

In the fourth couplet, "عاشقی را که چنین بادهٔ شبگیر دهند" (To a lover given such a predawn wine), Hafez argues that any true lover, given such intoxicating wine before dawn, would naturally become a worshiper of wine. This metaphor suggests that the intense experiences of love and divine ecstasy are irresistible and transformative.

In the fifth couplet, "برو ای زاهد و بر دُردکشان خرده مگیر" (Go away, O ascetic, and do not blame the wine-drinkers), Hafez admonishes the pious ascetic not to criticize the wine-drinkers. He reminds us that during the primordial covenant (روز الست), nothing else was promised but this gift of intoxicating love and ecstasy.

In the sixth couplet, "آن چه او ریخت به پیمانهٔ ما نوشیدیم" (What He poured into our cup, we drank), Hafez declares that whatever the divine has poured into their cup, be it the wine of paradise or intoxicating wine, they have consumed it all. This reflects a deep acceptance and gratitude for whatever experiences, joys, and sorrows the divine has bestowed upon them.

In the seventh couplet, "خندهٔ جامِ می و زلفِ گرهگیر نگار" (The laughter of the wine cup and the tangled hair of the beloved), Hafez juxtaposes the joyful laughter of the wine cup with the tangled hair of the beloved. He acknowledges that many vows, including his own, have been broken in the face of such overwhelming beauty and joy, reflecting the human tendency to break promises when confronted with intense emotions and desires.

We behold as Hafez masterfully intertwines themes of love, beauty, divine intoxication, and the human condition. Through vivid imagery and profound reflections, he captures the complexities and paradoxes of the spiritual and earthly experiences of love, urging the reader to embrace the transformative power of these emotions.

COMMENTARY ON TERMINOLOGY

This beautiful ghazal uses rich imagery and emotional depth, depicting a scene of intimate night-time revelry and introspection. The poem vividly describes a figure, possibly a beloved, who appears disheveled yet charming, drunk and joyous, entering the speaker's room at midnight. This figure brings with them an air of seductive mischief, holding a wine flask and singing sorrowfully close to the speaker's ear, questioning if the speaker, a long-time lover, is asleep.

The imagery is intense with contrasts: the tangled hair and the laughing, intoxicating mouth of the figure, suggesting a celebration of life and love, despite the late hour. Hafez uses this setup to explore themes of devotion and spirituality, contrasting the lover's hedonistic approach to life with the more abstinent and critical stance of the ascetic (referred to as "زاهد" or "zahed").

The poem then moves into a philosophical reflection about the nature of the divine gifts bestowed during the primordial "Day of Alast" (روز السّت), a Quranic reference to when souls acknowledged God's lordship before being born. The speaker implies that they partake in whatever is given to them, be it the wine of paradise or earthly intoxication, blurring the lines between sacred and profane.

The poem concludes with a reminder of the fleeting nature of resolutions, like the often-broken vows of the poet Hafez himself, illustrating the human struggle between spiritual aspirations and earthly desires. It reflects on the complex dance between divine love and worldly pleasure.

CHAPTER 47
GHAZAL 27: COME BACK TO ME, SO IT RETURNS

در دیرِ مغان آمد، یارم قدحی در دست
مست از می و میخواران از نرگس مستش مست

در نعلِ سمندِ او شکلِ مهِ نو پیدا
وز قدِ بلندِ او بالای صنوبر پست

آخر به چه گویم هست از خود خبرم، چون نیست
وز بهر چه گویم نیست با وی نظرم، چون هست

شمع دل دمسازم، بنشست چو او برخاست

و افغان ز نظربازان، برخاست چو او بنشست

گر غالیه خوش بو شد، در گیسوی او پیچید
ور وَسمه کمانکش گشت، در ابروی او پیوست

بازآی که بازآید عمر شدهٔ حافظ
هر چند که ناید باز، تیری که بشد از شست

GHAZAL 27: COME BACK TO ME, SO IT RETURNS

In the Magi's monastery, my beloved came, goblet in hand, I, Intoxicated, I must confess

I, Drunken with wine, and others fell drunk from her narcissus eyes, I must confess.

In the hoofprint of Her white steed, the shape of a new moon seen, And by Her lofty stature, the tall pine seems less, I must confess.

How can I speak of His being, when I am no longer aware of myself And why claim She is non-being, when I see Her in my presence, I must confess?

The candle of my heart, sits when She rises, And the cries of the flirtatious ones rise when she sits down, I must confess.

If the perfume becomes fragrant, it's because it entwined with Her hair, And if the eyeliner draws bows, it joins in her brows, I must confess.

Come back, so that the spent life of Hafez might return again,
Though an arrow released from the bow never comes back, I must confess.

COMMENTARY

In the first couplet, "قدحی در دست" (goblet in hand), Hafez describes his beloved entering the Magi's monastery with a goblet in hand, symbolizing intoxication and divine ecstasy. The beloved's presence and the intoxicating wine create a scene where Hafez and others are rendered drunk not only by the wine but also by the beloved's narcissus-like eyes. This imagery conveys the overwhelming allure and spiritual influence of the beloved, who transcends ordinary beauty and induces a state of mystical rapture.

In the second couplet, "شکلِ مهِ نو پیدا" (shape of a new moon seen), Hafez compares the hoofprint of the beloved's white steed to the shape of a new moon, suggesting a celestial and ethereal quality. The beloved's tall and majestic stature makes even the lofty pine seem insignificant in comparison. This highlights the beloved's unparalleled grace and the way her presence diminishes all else, symbolizing divine beauty and the awe it inspires.

In the third couplet, "از خود خبرم، چون نیست" (I am no longer aware of myself), Hafez grapples with the paradox of existence and non-existence in the presence of the beloved. He cannot speak of his own being when he is utterly absorbed in the beloved, losing all self-awareness. Conversely, he cannot claim the beloved is non-existent when she is so vividly present to him. This couplet captures the mystical experience of losing oneself in divine love, where personal identity and the beloved's presence blur into one.

In the fourth couplet, "شمع دل دمسازم" **(The candle of my heart),** Hafez describes the dynamic between his heart and the beloved. When the beloved rises, the candle of his heart, symbolizing his soul or inner light, sits in reverence. Conversely, the cries of the flirtatious ones rise when she sits down, indicating their yearning and admiration. This interplay reflects the profound impact the beloved has on the hearts of her admirers, illustrating her commanding and enchanting presence.

In the fifth couplet, "در گیسوی او پیچید" **(entwined with her hair),** Hafez attributes the fragrance of perfume and the shape of the eyeliner's bow to their association with the beloved's hair and brows. The beloved's beauty is so potent that it enhances and transforms everything it touches, symbolizing the elevating and intoxicating power of divine love and beauty.

In the final couplet, "بازآی" **(Come back),** Hafez implores the beloved to return so that his spent life might be revived. He acknowledges, however, that like an arrow released from a bow, time and moments lost cannot come back. This reflects the longing and despair of unfulfilled love, as well as the hope for renewal through the beloved's return, emphasizing the transient yet deeply impactful nature of love and life.

This is an invitation to the reader to contemplate the deeper truths of existence and the transformative power of divine love.

COMMENTARY ON TERMINOLOGY

The "دیر مغان" (Der-e Moghan), often referred to as the "Mystics' Tavern" or "Sufi Lodge," is a recurring symbol in Persian poetry and Sufi litera-ture. In both literal and metaphorical senses, it holds profound signifi-cance in the realm of Sufism, philosophy, and literature.

Physical and Symbolic Space: In a physical sense, the "دیر مغان" could be an actual gathering place or lodge where Sufis would meet for spiritual discussions, poetry recitations, and the consumption of wine as a symbol of divine intoxication. Symbolically, it represents a sacred space where seekers of truth and lovers of the Divine gather to explore the mysteries of existence, love, and spirituality.

Spiritual Journey: The "دیر مغان" serves as a metaphor for the spiritual journey. Sufism emphasizes moving beyond the surface of religious rituals and delving into the deeper, inner dimensions of faith. It repre-sents the inner sanctum of the heart, where the seeker's soul longs to be in union with the Divine, transcending the material world.

Unity and Intoxication: Wine, often associated with divine love and spiritual intoxication in Sufi poetry, is a recurring element within the "دیر مغان." It symbolizes the ecstatic state of union with the Divine, where the boundaries of self dissolve, and the seeker experiences a sense of unity and divine presence.

The Beloved: The "دیر مغان" is where the seeker encounters the Beloved, who can represent God or the ultimate Truth. This encounter is marked by love, yearning, and the passionate pursuit of spiritual enlightenment.

Community and Guidance: Within the "دیر مغان," Sufis often find a community of like-minded individuals and a spiritual guide or mentor (a Sheikh or Pir) who leads them on their path of spiritual realization. The guidance provided in this space is essential for the seeker's progress.

Literary Inspiration: The "دیر مغان" has been a rich source of inspiration for Persian poets like Hafez, Rumi, Attar, and others. It provides them with a setting to explore complex philosophical and metaphysical ideas through the medium of poetry. It's in this space that they often articulate their love for the Divine, their experiences of spiritual ecstasy, and their yearning for a deeper understanding of existence.

So, the "دیر مغان" is not merely a physical place but a deeply symbolic and spiritual concept that encapsulates the Sufi journey, the pursuit of divine knowledge, and the transformative power of love and intoxication in Persian literature and Sufi philosophy. It serves as a meeting point between earthly existence and the Divine realm, where seekers aim to transcend the material world and attain spiritual enlightenment.

CHAPTER 48
GHAZAL 28: THE PRAYER OF POWER

به جانِ خواجه و حقِ قدیم و عهدِ درست
که مونسِ دمِ صبحم، دعای دولت توست

سرشک من که ز طوفان نوح دست بَرَد
ز لوح سینه نیارَست نقشِ مهرِ تو شُست

بکن معامله‌ای، وین دل شکسته بخر
که با شکستگی ارزد به صد هزار درست

زبان مور به آصف دراز گشت و رواست

که خواجه خاتَمِ جم، یاوه کرد و باز نَجُست

دلا طمع مَبر از لطف بی‌نهایت دوست
چو لاف عشق زدی سر بباز، چابک و چُست

به صدق کوش، که خورشید زایَد از نَفَسَت
که از دروغ سیه روی گشت صبحِ نخست

شدم ز دست تو شیدای کوه و دشت و هنوز
نمی‌کنی به ترحم، نِطاقِ سلسله سست

مرنج حافظ و از دلبران جفاظ مجوی
گناه باغ چه باشد چو این گیاه نَرُست

GHAZAL 28: THE PRAYER OF POWER

By the life of the master, the ancient vow, and the truth we hold,
   Your prayer's power at the breath of dawn, is your companion, truth be told.

My tears have surpassed the flood of Noah, but they could not wash away
   the mark of your love from the tablet of my heart, it continued to hold

Make a trade, take this heart, though broken apart,
   Even shattered, it's worth a hundred whole, truth be told.

The ant's voice reached Solomon, just as it's told,
   For Jamshid's ring he lost, never again to behold.

Heart, don't abuse the benevolence of the friend's endless grace,
   When you boast of love, risk all, be brave and bold.

Strive for truth, let the sun rise from your breath,
   For falsehood darkened the dawn's first light, truth be told.

Because of you, I'm enamored with the mountains and plains, and yet
    you do not, out of compassion, loosen the chain of bondage, for me
to roam

Do not be upset, Hafez, and do not seek refuge in the beloved
    What is the fault of the garden if a plant does not grow?

COMMENTARY

This is a reflection on the themes of love, divine grace, and the spiritual journey. Each couplet delves into profound truths about human experience and the relationship with the divine, interwoven with rich imagery and deep emotion.

In the first couplet, "دعای دولت توست" (the prayer for your prosperity), Hafez swears by the life of his master, the eternal truth, and the ancient covenant that his morning companion is the prayer for the beloved's prosperity. This emphasizes the poet's devotion and the spiritual practice of praying for the well-being of the beloved, symbolizing a selfless love that transcends personal desires.

In the second couplet, "سرشک من" (my tear), Hafez compares his tear, which could rival the deluge of Noah's flood, to the indelible mark of the beloved's love etched on his heart. Despite the powerful forces that might attempt to erase it, this love remains unwashed from the tablet of his heart. This imagery conveys the permanence and depth of Hafez's affection, suggesting that true love is resilient and enduring.

In the third couplet, "دل شکسته" (broken heart), Hafez asks for a transaction where the beloved buys his broken heart, asserting that even in its broken state, it is worth a hundred thousand whole ones.

This reflects the Sufi notion that spiritual brokenness and humility are more valuable than worldly perfection, emphasizing the worth and beauty found in vulnerability and openness.

In the fourth couplet, "زبان مور به آصف" (the ant's tongue to Asaf), Hafez references the story of Solomon (Asaf) and the ant, suggesting that it is appropriate for even the smallest of creatures to speak out to great wisdom. The master's failure to seek the lost ring of Jamshid, symbolizing lost wisdom or power, underscores the importance of humility and the recognition that even the greatest can make mistakes. This encourages a recognition of the value in all voices and perspectives.

In the fifth couplet, "لطف بی‌نهایت دوست" (the boundless grace of the friend), Hafez advises not to lose hope in the infinite grace of the divine. He urges that once one professes love, they must be ready to sacrifice everything swiftly and nimbly. This reflects the Sufi path of surrender and the ultimate commitment to the divine love that requires total self-abandonment.

In the sixth couplet, "صدق" (truthfulness), Hafez emphasizes the importance of truthfulness, suggesting that through sincere effort, the breath of the seeker can give birth to the sun (enlightenment). He contrasts this with the darkness that arises from lies, indicating that the pursuit of truth leads to spiritual illumination, while falsehood brings darkness and disgrace.

In the seventh couplet, "شیدای کوه و دشت" (mad for the mountains and deserts), Hafez laments his madness for the wilderness, driven by his love for the beloved, who remains unyielding and unsympathetic. This couplet expresses the poet's deep yearning and the emotional toll of unrequited love, portraying the beloved's aloofness and the intense passion that drives him to the extremes of nature.

In the final couplet, "گناه باغ چه باشد" (what is the garden's sin), Hafez advises against seeking faults in lovers and cautions against harboring resentment. He uses the metaphor of a garden where some plants may not grow, implying that just as it is not the garden's fault if certain plants do not flourish, it is unjust to blame or judge the beloved for the complexities of love. This suggests acceptance and a broader perspective on the nature of love and human relationships.

Hafez's ghazal masterfully intertwines themes of divine love, human vulnerability, and spiritual truth. Through his eloquent use of imagery and metaphor, he conveys the complexities of the spiritual journey and the transformative power of love and devotion.

CHAPTER 49
GHAZAL 29: GOING WITH THE TIMES

ما را ز خیال تو چه پروای شراب است؟

خُم گو سر خود گیر، که خُمخانه خراب است

گر خَمر بهشت است بریزید که بی دوست

هر شربت عَذبَم که دهی، عین عذاب است

افسوس که شُد دلبر و در دیدهٔ گریان

تحریرِ خیالِ خطِ او نقشِ بر آب است

بیدار شو ای دیده که ایمن نتوان بود

زین سیل دمادم که در این منزل خواب است

معشوق عیان می‌گذرد بر تو، ولیکن
اغیار همی‌بیند از آن بسته نقاب است

گل بر رخ رنگین تو تا لطف عرق دید
در آتش شوق از غم دل، غرق گلاب است

سبز است در و دشت بیا تا نگذاریم
دست از سر آبی که جهان جمله سراب است

در کُنجِ دِماغم مطلب جای نصیحت
کاین گوشه پر از زمزمهٔ چنگ و رَباب است

حافظ چه شد ار عاشق و رند است و نظرباز
بس طورِ عجب، لازم ایام شباب است

GHAZAL 29: GOING WITH THE TIMES

With dreams of you, what need for earthly wine is there?
    Forget the grapes and goblets, only love divine is there.

Though heavens tempt with nectar, pour it out, my love's away,
    No joy in earthly pleasures when my soul is pining, is there?

Alas, your form is now a mirage, shimmering in tearful sight,
    Each promised word a fleeting echo, nothing not lost in time's design, is there?

Awaken, eyes, from slumber, for is no safety
    from this relentless deluge, in this house of dreams, is there?

My love parades before me, very explicit, but to stranger's eyes
    completely veiled, no chance to see its face, is there?

When the rose saw upon your colorful face, the grace of fragrant dew, passion's fire,
    and sorrow of its heart, there is nothing not immersed in rosewater is there?

The world's a fleeting mirage, come drink, while meadows gleam,
    But what is joy without you, in this world of pain and care, is there?

The fields are lush and green, come my love, let's not forego any
mirage
    while yet we may, for there is nothing in this world that is not a
mirage, is there?

In the corners of the streets of my mind, don't seek wisdom or advice
    For there is nothing but the sweet sound of harp and lute, is there?

What if I'm lost and reckless, eyes that wander, heart aflame,
    What is left of youth's entitlement, but to love and despair, is there?

What if Hafez is a lover, a *Rend*, wine-imbibing, and free with his gaze?
    A kaleidoscope of vibrant ways, what else but the *time of youth* is
there?

COMMENTARY

In the first couplet, "خیال تو" (thoughts of you), Hafez declares that his thoughts of the beloved overshadow any desire for wine. The image of the wine jar taking care of itself because the wine cellar is ruined underscores his indifference to earthly pleasures when consumed by the beloved's memory.

It begins with the speaker expressing his indifference to wine, as he is consumed by thoughts of his beloved. He says that even the wine of paradise would be torture without his beloved.

In the second couplet, "خَمر بهشت" (wine of paradise), Hafez boldly states that even the wine of paradise holds no allure without the beloved. He expresses that any sweet drink given without the presence of the beloved becomes sheer torment, emphasizing the beloved's irreplaceable value.

The narrator bemoans the absence of his beloved. He says that his tearful eyes can only see the image of his beloved's handwriting, which is like a mirage.

In the third couplet, "نقش بر آب" (writing on water), he laments the departure of the beloved, whose image in his tear-filled eyes becomes like writing on water, ephemeral and fleeting. This metaphor poignantly captures the anguish of unfulfilled longing and the impermanence of memories.

The speaker urges his eye to wake up and face reality. He says that he cannot be safe in this house of sleep, where his beloved is gone.

In the fourth couplet, "سیل دمادم" (relentless flood), Hafez urges vigilance, warning that one cannot feel secure in this dwelling due to the relentless flood. This flood symbolizes the constant threat of sorrow and change, reminding us of life's uncertainties and the need to remain alert.

His beloved passes by him openly, but others can only see him because he is veiled.

In the fifth couplet, "بسته نقاب" (veiled), Hafez observes that although the beloved passes by openly, she remains veiled to outsiders. This suggests that true beauty and love are apparent only to those who truly see, while others remain oblivious.

Here the poet compares the rose on his beloved's cheek to a rose that has been drowned in rosewater from the fire of longing for the sorrow of his heart.

In the sixth couplet, "لطف عرق" (grace of your sweat), he describes how the sight of the beloved's sweat makes the rose on her face weep in longing. This vivid imagery conveys the intensity of desire and the beauty that incites such profound emotions.

The poet invites his beloved to come to the green door and meadow. He says that they should not let go of the water, for the world is all a mirage.

In the seventh couplet, "جهان جمله سراب" (world full of mirages), Hafez invites the beloved to enjoy the green fields and plains, urging not to abandon the refreshing presence of water in a world full of mirages. This highlights the preciousness of true experiences amid life's illusions.

There is no room for advice in the corner of his heart. He says that this corner is full of the murmur of the lute and the rebab.

In the eighth couplet, "نصیحت" (advice), he dismisses the idea of heeding advice, noting that his mind is filled with the music of the harp and lute. This reflects his preference for the joy and distraction of music over sober counsel, emphasizing his embrace of life's pleasures.

The speaker says that it does not matter if he is a lover, a rake, and a gazer. He says that these are all strange things, but they are necessary for the days of youth.

In the final couplet, "عاشق و رند" (lover and libertine), Hafez defends his lifestyle, stating that being a lover, a rogue, and an observer is fitting for the days of youth. This unapologetic stance highlights the value he places on experiencing life fully and authentically.

Hafez's ghazal masterfully intertwines the themes of love, longing, and the search for deeper meaning beyond worldly pleasures. Through rich imagery and poignant reflections, he captures the complexities of human emotions and the transformative power of love and beauty.

Commentary 2

CHAPTER 50
GHAZAL 30: YOUR HAIR HAS BOUND A THOUSAND HEARTS

زلفت هزار دل به یکی تار مو ببست
راه هزار چاره‌گر از چار سو ببست

تا عاشقان به بوی نسیمش دهند جان
بگشود نافه‌ای و دَرِ آرزو ببست

شیدا از آن شدم که نگارم چو ماه نو
ابرو نمود و جلوه‌گری کرد و رو ببست

ساقی به چند رنگ، می اندر پیاله ریخت

این نقش‌ها نگر، که چه خوش در کدو ببست

یا رب چه غمزه کرد صُراحی که خون خُم
با نعره‌های قُلقُلش اندر گلو ببست

مطرب چه پرده ساخت که در پردهٔ سماع
بر اهل وجد و حال، در های و هو ببست

حافظ! هر آن که عشق نَورزید و وصل خواست
احرامِ طوفِ کعبهٔ دل بی وضو ببست

GHAZAL 30: YOUR HAIR HAS BOUND A THOUSAND HEARTS

Your hair has bound a thousand hearts with a single strand.
  Closed off paths of a thousand problem-solvers from all directions **with a single strand.**

So that lovers may give their lives for the scent of the Beloved in the breeze.
  They opened a musk pod and closed the door of desire **with a single strand.**

I became enamored because my beloved, like the new moon...
  ...showed their eyebrows, displayed their charms, and then hid their face **with a single strand.**

The cupbearer poured wine of many colors into the cup.
  Look at these patterns, how beautifully they are bound in the gourd **with a single strand.**

Oh Lord, what a wink the wine jug gave that the blood of the wine...
  ...with its gurgling cries, got stuck in its throat **with a single strand.**

What a melody the musician created that in the veil of the spiritual dance...

...closed the doors of ecstasy and rapture to those in a state of joy and ecstasy **with a single strand.**

Hafez! Whoever did not cultivate love and desired union...

...tied the ritual garment of circling the Kaaba of their heart without ablution **with a single strand.**

COMMENTARY

In the first couplet, "زلفت هزار دل" (your tresses), Hafez speaks of the beloved's tresses that bind a thousand hearts with a single strand. He illustrates the power and allure of the beloved's hair, which captivates and ensnares many. The phrase also suggests that the beloved's beauty is so compelling that it confounds even the most skilled problem-solvers from all directions.

In the second couplet, "بوی نسیمش" (scent of her breeze), Hafez describes how lovers sacrifice their lives for the mere scent of the beloved's breeze. The beloved opens a perfumed pouch and closes the door of desire, symbolizing the fleeting yet intoxicating experience of her presence, which leaves lovers yearning for more.

In the third couplet, "نگارم چو ماه نو" (my beloved like the new moon), Hafez becomes infatuated when his beloved, like a new moon, reveals her eyebrow and then hides her face. This imagery reflects the tantalizing nature of the beloved's beauty, which appears briefly and then disappears, leaving the lover in a state of longing and fascination.

In the fourth couplet, "می اندر پیاله" (wine in the cup), Hafez observes the cupbearer pouring wine into the goblet in various colors. He marvels at how beautifully these images are contained within the wine jug, indicating the multi-faceted nature of beauty and pleasure, and how they can be artistically and intricately presented.

In the fifth couplet, "غمزه صُراحى" (the flirtation of the flask), Hafez wonders about the flirtation of the wine flask that causes the wine jar's blood to be stopped in its throat with the gurgling sound. This personification and imagery emphasize the seductive and almost dangerous allure of the wine, likening it to the beloved's captivating charms.

In the sixth couplet, "پردهٔ سماع" (musical performance), Hafez questions what melody the musician played that, during the musical performance, closed the door of noise and commotion for those in spiritual ecstasy. This suggests that the music had a profound, calming effect on the audience, transporting them to a state of inner peace and contemplation.

In the final couplet, "عشق نَورزید" (did not love), Hafez states that anyone who does not love but seeks union without love has tied the pilgrim's cloth of the heart's Kaaba without ablution. This implies that true union and spiritual fulfillment require sincere love and purity of intention, rather than mere ritualistic acts.

Hafez's ghazal weaves and reflects the complexities of human emotions and the transformative power of love, inviting readers to contemplate the deeper truths of existence and the profound impact of divine beauty.

CHAPTER 51
GHAZAL 143: FOR YEARS MY HEART SOUGHT SECRETS

سال‌ها دل طلبِ جامِ جم از ما می‌کرد
وآنچه خود داشت ز بیگانه تمنّا می‌کرد

گوهری کز صدفِ کون و مکان بیرون است
طلب از گمشدگانِ لبِ دریا می‌کرد

مشکلِ خویش بَرِ پیرِ مُغان بُردم دوش
کاو به تأییدِ نظر حلِّ معما می‌کرد

· · ·

دیدمش خُرَّم و خندان قدحِ باده به دست
واندر آن آینه صد گونه تماشا می‌کرد

گفتم این جامِ جهان‌بین به تو کی داد حکیم؟
گفت آن روز که این گنبدِ مینا می‌کرد

بی‌دلی در همه‌احوالِ خدا با او بود
او نمی‌دیدش و از دور خدا را می‌کرد

این‌همه شعبدهٔ خویش که می‌کرد اینجا
سامری پیشِ عصا و یدِ بیضا می‌کرد

گفت آن یار کز او گشت سرِ دار بلند
جُرمش این بود که اسرار هویدا می‌کرد

فیضِ روحُ‌القُدُس ار باز مدد فرماید

دیگران هم بکنند آنچه مسیحا می‌کرد

گفتمش سلسلهٔ زلفِ بُتان از پیِ چیست
گفت حافظ گله‌ای از دلِ شیدا می‌کرد

GHAZAL 143: FOR YEARS MY HEART SOUGHT SECRETS

FOR YEARS, my heart sought the Cup of Jamshid from me,
　　And craved from strangers what it already possessed, is the secret.

A jewel that transcends the shell of time and space,
　　It sought from those lost by the shore of the sea looking for secrets.

A jewel that transcends the shell of time and space, He sought from those lost by the shore of the sea.

Last night, I brought my problem to the Magian elder,
　　Who, with the affirmation of insight, unraveled the secret.

I saw him joyful and smiling, wine cup in hand,
　　In that mirror, he beheld a hundred wonders and secrets.

I asked, "When did the sage bestow upon you this world-seeing cup?"

He replied, "On the day he crafted this azure dome." That is no secret.

In every possible state, the heart was one with God, And yet thought it could not see Him and sought God elsewhere. That is the secret.

All these tricks he performed here, were like Samiri
    before the staff and the radiant hand, that is the secret.

He said, "That friend whose head rose high on the gallows,
    His crime was revealing the hidden secrets ."

If the Holy Spirit again might bestow grace,
    Others can do what the Messiah did. This is the secret.

I asked him, "What is the reason for the tresses of the beauties?"
    He said, "Hafez lamented the plight of the passionate heart." That is a secret.

CHAPTER 52
COMMENTARY

CHAPTER 53
GHAZAL 152: YOUR BEAUTY SET THE WORLD ON FIRE

ALI ARSANJANI

در ازل پرتوِ حُسنت ز تجلی دَم زد-
عشق پیدا شد و آتش به همه عالم زد

جلوه‌ای کرد رُخَت دید مَلَک عشق نداشت
عینِ آتش شد از این غیرت و بر آدم زد

عقل می‌خواست کز آن شعله چراغ افروزد
برق غیرت بدرخشید و جهان برهم زد

مدعی خواست که آید به تماشاگهِ راز

دست غیب آمد و بر سینهٔ نامحرم زد

دیگران قرعهٔ قسمت همه بر عیش زدند
دل غمدیدهٔ ما بود که هم بر غم زد

جانِ عِلْوی هوس چاهِ زنخدان تو داشت
دست در حلقهٔ آن زلفِ خَم اندر خَم زد

حافظ آن روز طربنامهٔ عشق تو نوشت
که قلم بر سرِ اسبابِ دلِ خُرَّم زد

GHAZAL 152: YOUR BEAUTY SET THE WORLD ON FIRE

At the dawn of time, the ray of your beauty appeared and shined forth
    Love appeared and set the whole world on fire as it **shined forth**

Your face appeared, the angel of love saw it and could not bear it
    Like fire in his protective jealousy, struck Adam and **shined forth**

Reason wanted to light a lamp with that flame, but the lightening
    of protective jealousy upset the world in a flash and **shined forth**

The pretender tried to gain access to the Observatory of Secrets
    The Hand of the Unseen struck the contender and **shined forth**

Others gambled their share on the happy ignorance of hedonism
    It was our sorrow felt heart that cast it aside and **shined forth**

The lofty soul longed for the indentation of your chin and put his fingers
    in the tresses of those curly locks and **shined forth**

Hafez wrote the letter proclaiming your love that day
  When he put the pen to the head of the happy heart and it let **shine forth**

CHAPTER 54
COMMENTARY

HAFEZ'S GHAZAL is a profound exploration of the origins of love and beauty, the conflict between divine and worldly knowledge, and the ultimate triumph of spiritual love over temporal concerns. Each couplet is rich with metaphors and allegories, painting a vivid picture of the mystical journey.

In the first couplet, "پرتو حُسنت ز تجلی دَم زد" (the radiance of your beauty shone forth at the beginning), Hafez describes the moment of creation when the divine beauty revealed itself. This revelation gave birth to love, which set the entire world ablaze. The imagery of fire signifies the transformative and consuming power of divine love, which permeates and ignites all of existence.

In the second couplet, "رخَت دید مَلَک عشق نداشت" (the angel saw your face and did not possess love), Hafez narrates how the angel, upon witnessing the divine beauty, realized its lack of love. The angel's envy and intense reaction turned into pure fire and struck Adam, symbolizing the introduction of divine love to humanity and the inherent jealousy and desire it brings.

In the third couplet, "عقل می‌خواست کز آن شعله چراغ افروزد" (reason wanted to light a lamp from that flame), reason attempted to harness the flame of divine love for enlightenment. However, the lightning of divine jealousy (غیرت) flashed and disrupted the world, indicating that true divine love and knowledge are beyond the grasp of mere rationality and intellect, causing upheaval in the process.

In the fourth couplet, "تماشاگهِ راز" (the theater of secrets), a claimant (مدعی) wished to enter the theater of divine mysteries. However, a hidden hand (دستِ غیب) struck the chest of the uninitiated, barring them from the sacred secrets. This emphasizes that divine knowledge and experiences are reserved for those who are spiritually prepared and pure, excluding the unworthy.

In the fifth couplet, "قرعهٔ قسمت همه بر عیش زدند" (others cast their lots for joy), Hafez contrasts the fate of others, who sought and obtained worldly pleasures, with his own sorrowful heart, which consistently encountered grief. This highlights the poet's acceptance of suffering as part of his spiritual journey and his belief that true love often comes with pain.

In the sixth couplet, "جانِ عِلْوی هوسِ چاهِ زنخدان تو داشت" (the celestial soul desired the dimple of your chin), Hafez illustrates the celestial soul's yearning for the beloved's beauty, represented by the dimple on the chin and the curly locks. The hand reaching into the curls signifies the soul's attempt to connect with the divine, showing the intense desire and the complexity of the beloved's allure.

In the final couplet, "طربنامهٔ عشق تو نوشت" (the song of your love was written), Hafez reveals that he composed the joyful song of the beloved's love on the day he decided to abandon worldly attachments. The metaphor of the pen striking the joyous heart symbolizes the creative and transformative power of divine love, which inspired him to produce his poetic works.

Hafez's ghazal intricately weaves themes of the mystical journey, where divine love ignites the soul, disrupts worldly knowledge, and ultimately leads to spiritual enlightenment and creative expression.

CHAPTER 55
GHAZAL 374: LET'S CRAFT A NEW DESIGN

بیا تا گل برافشانیم و می در ساغر اندازیم-
فلک را سقف بشکافیم و طرحی نو دراندازیم

اگر غم لشکر انگیزد که خون عاشقان ریزد

من و ساقی به هم تازیم و بنیادش براندازیم

شراب ارغوانی را گلاب اندر قدح ریزیم
نسیم عطرگردان را شِکَر در مجمر اندازیم

چو در دست است رودی خوش بزن مطرب سرودی خوش
که دست افشان غزل خوانیم و پاکوبان سر اندازیم

صبا خاک وجود ما بدان عالی جناب انداز
بود کان شاه خوبان را نظر بر منظر اندازیم

یکی از عقل می‌لافد یکی طامات می‌بافد
بیا کاین داوری‌ها را به پیش داور اندازیم

بهشت عدن اگر خواهی بیا با ما به میخانه
که از پای خمت روزی به حوض کوثر اندازیم

سخندانیّ و خوش‌خوانی نمی‌ورزند در شیراز
بیا حافظ که تا خود را به ملکی دیگر اندازیم

GHAZAL 374: LET'S CRAFT A NEW DESIGN

COME SCATTER FLOWERS, cast wine into goblets for a new design
    tear the ceiling of the sky at the seams and craft a new design

If sorrow were even to think to raise an army to shed the blood of lovers
    Saghi the winebearer and I will join and uproot its foundations with a new design

We will pour rosewater into the glistening chalice of crimson wine,
    cast sugar into the incense so the breeze brings winding fragrances with a new design

If you have a lute in hand then play us a melodious tune, O musician,
    For we will sing along a ghazal poetry, nod and step to the beat in a new design

. . .

If we are but dust to the breeze, let us be cast to that noble presence, In hopes that the king of beauty gazes upon our reflection with a new design.

One boasts of reason, another weaves tales of mystical boasts, Come, let us bring these judgments before the ultimate arbiter with a new design.

If you seek the Eden of bliss, join us in the tavern, Where from the foot of the cask, one day, we'll cast ourselves into the pool of Kauthar with a new design.

In Shiraz, eloquence and sweet singing are no longer cherished, Come, Hafez, let us cast ourselves into a new realm with a new design.

COMMENTARY

Hafez's ghazal "بیا تا گل برافشانیم و می در ساغر اندازیم" is a passionate call to celebrate life, break free from conventional limitations, and embrace the transformative power of love and joy. This celebration of life, love, and the transformative power of joy. Each couplet is a call to break free from conventional limitations, embrace the beauty and pleasure of the world, and seek a higher, more ecstatic state of being through love and celebration. Through rich imagery and passionate appeals, Hafez encourages the reader to join him in a journey of joyous transcendence.

In the first couplet, "گل برافشانیم" (scatter flowers), Hafez invites the reader to join him in celebrating life with flowers and wine. The phrase "طرحی نو دراندازیم" (create a new design) emphasizes the desire to break free from the constraints of the ordinary and create something innovative and beautiful, challenging the very fabric of the heavens.

In the second couplet, "غم لشکر انگیزد" (sorrow raises an army), Hafez declares that if sorrow threatens to overwhelm lovers, he and the cupbearer will unite to overthrow its foundation. This reflects the resilience of love and the determination to combat despair with unity and joy.

In the third couplet, "شراب ارغوانی" (crimson wine), Hafez describes the sensory pleasures of combining the rich colors and fragrances of wine and rosewater. The addition of "شِکَر در مجمر" (sugar to the incense burner) enhances the sweetness and aroma, symbolizing the heightening of life's pleasures through sensory indulgence.

In the fourth couplet, "خوش رودی" (sweet melody), Hafez urges the minstrel to play joyful music so they can dance and sing with abandon. The imagery of hand-clapping and head-tossing while singing underscores the communal joy and the spontaneous celebration of life.

In the fifth couplet, "صبا خاک وجود" (breeze, carry the dust), Hafez asks the morning breeze to take their essence to the beloved. The hope is that the "شاه خوبان" (king of beauties) will cast a favorable glance upon them, symbolizing the longing for divine or beloved attention and approval.

In the sixth couplet, "عقل می‌لافد" (boasts of reason), Hafez criticizes those who argue over rationality and mysticism. He suggests bringing these disputes before the ultimate judge, implying that true wisdom transcends these earthly debates and is found in divine understanding.

In the seventh couplet, "بهشت عدن" (Garden of Eden), Hafez equates the tavern with paradise. He asserts that the ecstasy found in the tavern, symbolized by the wine jar, can lead to the heavenly pool of Kawthar. This suggests that spiritual bliss can be attained through earthly joys.

In the final couplet, "سخندانیّ و خوشخوانی" (eloquence and sweet singing), Hafez laments the lack of appreciation for eloquence and melody in his hometown. He invites the reader to leave with him to another realm where their talents and joys can be fully appreciated and celebrated.

CHAPTER 56
GHAZAL 276: A DISCOURSE WITH THE ROSE

باغبان گر پنج‌روزی صحبتِ گل بایدش-
بر جفایِ خارِ هجران صبر بلبل بایدش

ای دل اندر بندِ زلفش از پریشانی مَنال
مرغِ زیرک چون به دام افتد تحمل بایدش

رندِ عالم‌سوز را با مصلحت‌بینی چه‌کار
کار مُلک است آن که تدبیر و تأمل بایدش

تکیه بر تقوی و دانش در طریقت کافریست

راهرو گر صد هنر دارد توکل بایدش

با چُنین زلف و رُخَش بادا نظربازی حرام
هر که روی یاسمین و جَعدِ سنبل بایدش

نازها زان نرگسِ مستانه‌اش باید کشید
این دلِ شوریده تا آن جَعد و کاکُل بایدش

ساقیا در گردشِ ساغر تعلل تا به چند
دَور چون با عاشقان افتد تَسَلسُل بایدش

کیست حافظ تا ننوشد باده بی‌آوازِ رود
عاشقِ مسکین چرا چندین تجمل بایدش

GHAZAL 276: A DISCOURSE WITH THE ROSE

In the gardener's brief days, a discourse with the rose he needs,
   Against the thorns of separation, the nightingale's patience **he needs.**

O heart, caught in her tresses, lament not your disarray,
   Like a clever bird snared, endurance **he needs**.

What use has a world-burning libertine for prudence?
   The one who rules empires, strategy and reflection **he needs**.

To lean on piety and knowledge in the Sufi path is heresy,
   For the traveler, no matter his talents, faith in God **he needs**.

With such hair and face, to gaze with desire is forbidden,
   Anyone who beholds her jasmine face and curly locks, restraint **he needs.**

From those drunken, narcissus eyes, coquetry must be endured,
   This restless heart, to her curls and ringlets, is drawn—**he needs.**

O Sāqī, how long will you delay the wine's rounds?
When among lovers it circulates, continuity **he needs**.

Who is Hafez, that he might not drink the wine silent as the stream?
For the humble lover, why such adornment **he needs**?

COMMENTARY

Each couplet delves into the wisdom required to navigate the challenges and pleasures of life, offering profound insights into human behavior and divine guidance.

In the first couplet, "جفای خارِ هجران" (**the torment of separation's thorn**), Hafez compares the fleeting pleasure of a gardener enjoying the company of a flower for five days to the patience a nightingale must have when enduring the torment of separation from the flower due to the thorn. This metaphor highlights the transient nature of joy and the enduring pain of separation, suggesting that patience is essential to endure life's inevitable hardships.

In the second couplet, "بندِ زلفش" (**bond of her tresses**), Hafez advises the heart not to complain about the chaos caused by being entangled in the beloved's hair. He compares it to a clever bird that, once trapped, must endure its fate. This illustrates the idea that love often brings turmoil, but one must endure it gracefully.

In the third couplet, "رندِ عالمسوز" (**world-consuming libertine**), Hafez questions what a worldly-wise libertine has to do with prudence and careful consideration. He suggests that matters of state require planning and thought, implying that a true seeker or lover operates beyond such worldly concerns and calculations.

In the fourth couplet, "تکیه بر تقوی و دانش" (**relying on piety and**

knowledge), Hafez argues that relying solely on piety and knowledge in the path of spiritual enlightenment is heresy. Instead, he emphasizes that a traveler, regardless of their many skills, must have trust (توکل) in divine guidance. This underscores the importance of faith over mere intellectual or moral virtues in the spiritual journey.

In the fifth couplet, "زلف و رُخَش" (her tresses and face), Hafez laments that with such beauty, it should be forbidden to admire her face and tresses. He suggests that anyone who seeks the beauty of jasmine and the curls of hyacinth must endure prohibition, high-lighting the unattainability and divine nature of true beauty.

In the sixth couplet, "نازها زان نرگس مستانه‌اش" (the coquettish glances of her intoxicated narcissus-like eyes), Hafez states that one must endure the coquettish glances of her intoxicating eyes. He implies that the heart, though disturbed, desires the beauty of her curls and locks, emphasizing the persistent longing and turmoil that comes with love.

In the seventh couplet, "گردشِ ساغر" (the turning of the goblet), Hafez questions the cupbearer about the delay in passing the goblet. He insists that when it is the lovers' turn, there should be no hesitation, symbolizing the urgency and continuous cycle of love and intoxication.

In the final couplet, "باده بی‌آوازِ رود" (wine without the music of the harp), Hafez rhetorically asks who he is to refrain from drinking wine without the accompaniment of music. He wonders why a humble lover should seek such luxuries, suggesting that the true essence of love and joy does not require external adornments but lies in the simple, profound experience itself.

CHAPTER 57
REFERENCES

IN THIS SECTION I have provided an expanded reference that aims to provide a rather comprehensive overview of primary sources, translations, secondary literature, comparative studies, and digital resources related to Hafez of Shiraz. I include brief descriptions to give readers an idea of each source's focus or significance.

Primary Sources:

1 Hafez. "Divan-e Hafez" (Collection of Hafez's Poems). 14th century.

This is the original collection of Hafez's ghazals and other poetic forms in Persian.

Notable Translations:

1 Bell, G. (1897). "Poems from the Divan of Hafiz". London: Heinemann.

○ One of the earliest English translations, known for its Victorian-era interpretations.

2 Arberry, A.J. (1974). "Fifty Poems of Hafiz". Cambridge: Cambridge University Press.

○ A scholarly translation with extensive notes and commentary.

3 Ordoubadian, R. (2006). "The Poems of Hafez". Bethesda: Ibex Publishers.

° A modern translation aiming to capture both literal meaning and poetic essence.

4 Davis, D. (2019). "Faces of Love: Hafez and the Poets of Shiraz". New York: Penguin Classics.

° A recent translation placing Hafez in context with other Persian poets.

5 Avery, P. & Heath-Stubbs, J. (1952). "Hafiz of Shiraz: Thirty Poems". London: John Murray.

° A collaboration between a Persian scholar and an English poet.

Secondary Sources:

1 Lewisohn, L. (2010). "Hafiz and the Religion of Love in Classical Persian Poetry". London: I.B. Tauris.

° Explores the spiritual and mystical aspects of Hafez's poetry.

2 Loloi, P. (2004). "Hafiz, Master of Persian Poetry: A Critical Bibliography". London: I.B. Tauris.

° An extensive bibliography of works about Hafez and his poetry.

3 Khorramshahi, B. (2002). "Hafez-e Shirazi". Tehran: Tarh-e Now.

° A comprehensive study in Persian on Hafez's life and works.

4 Meisami, J.S. (1987). "Medieval Persian Court Poetry". Princeton: Princeton University Press.

° Provides historical and literary context for Hafez's poetry.

5 Schimmel, A. (1992). "A Two-Colored Brocade: The Imagery of Persian Poetry". Chapel Hill: University of North Carolina Press.

° Discusses the rich imagery in Persian poetry, including Hafez's work.

Comparative Studies:

1 Arberry, A.J. (1958). "Classical Persian Literature". London: George Allen & Unwin.

° Places Hafez within the broader context of Persian literature.

2 Yarshater, E. (1988). "Persian Literature". Albany: State University of New York Press.

° A comprehensive overview of Persian literature, including Hafez's contributions.

Digital Resources:

1 Ganjoor (https://ganjoor.net/hafez/)

◦ An online database of Persian poetry, including the complete works of Hafez in the original Persian.

2 The University of Chicago's "Printed Editions and Translations of Hafez" (https://persian.uchicago.edu/hafez-editions)

◦ A comprehensive list of printed editions and translations of Hafez's work.

- 3 Dr. Abdolkarim Soroush lectures on "the God of Rumi and the God of Hafez"

CHAPTER 58
FEEDBACK TO THE
AUTHOR

THE AUTHOR WOULD GREATLY APPRECIATE feedback by going to this website and filling out this form.
https://forms.gle/PtLpL2MBULQxm8ie6

SCAN ME

www.ingramcontent.com/pod-product-compliance
Lightning Source LLC
Chambersburg PA
CBHW030355030726
47497CB00002B/354